THE FILMS OF
SPIKE LEE
FIVE
FOR
FIVE
PHOTOGRAPHS BY
DAVID LEE

TERRY McMILLAN

TONI CADE BAMBARA

NELSON GEORGE

CHARLES JOHNSON

HENRY LOUIS GATES, JR.

FOREWORD BY
MELVIN VAN PEEBLES

INTRODUCTION BY
SPIKE LEE

STEWART, TABORI & CHANG
NEW YORK

Text copyright © 1991 Forty Acres and a Mule Filmworks, Inc.
Photographs copyright © 1991 Forty Acres and a Mule Filmworks, Inc.
"One Meaning of *Mo' Better Blues*" copyright © 1991 Charles Johnson
Photograph of Spike and David Lee, pages 8 and 10,
copyright © 1991 Sikay Tang

Published in 1991 by Stewart, Tabori & Chang, Inc.
575 Broadway, New York, New York 10012

LIBRARY OF CONGRESS CATALOGUING-IN-PUBLICATION DATA
Lee, Spike.
    Five for five : the films of Spike Lee / [essays by] Terry
McMillan . . . [et al.] ; photographs by David Lee ; foreword by
Melvin Van Peebles ; introduction by Spike Lee.
    ISBN 1-55670-216-7.—ISBN 1-55670-217-5 (pbk.)
    1. Lee, Spike—Criticism and interpretation.   2. Afro-Americans in
motion pictures.   3. Afro-Americans in the motion picture industry—
United States.   I. McMillan, Terry.   I. Title.   90-29025
PN1998.3L44A3   1991   CIP
791.43'75'0973—dc20

Distributed in the U.S. by Workman Publishing,
708 Broadway, New York, New York 10003
Distributed in Canada by Canadian Manda Group,
P.O. Box 920 Station U, Toronto, Ontario M8Z 5P9
Distributed in all other territories by
Little, Brown and Company, International Division,
34 Beacon Street, Boston, Massachusetts 02108

Manuscript editor: Shirley L. Poole

Printed in Japan
10 9 8 7 6 5 4 3 2 1

CONTENTS

RIGHT ON, AS IN RIGHT ON TIME   6
MELVIN VAN PEEBLES

PREFACE   9
DAVID LEE

FIVE FOR FIVE   11
SPIKE LEE

SHE'S GOTTA HAVE IT

THOUGHTS ON *SHE'S GOTTA HAVE IT*   19
TERRY McMILLAN
PHOTOGRAPHS   30

SCHOOL DAZE

PROGRAMMING WITH *SCHOOL DAZE*   47
TONI CADE BAMBARA
PHOTOGRAPHS   56

DO THE RIGHT THING

DO THE RIGHT THING: FILM AND FURY   77
NELSON GEORGE
PHOTOGRAPHS   82

MO' BETTER BLUES

ONE MEANING OF *MO' BETTER BLUES*   117
CHARLES JOHNSON
PHOTOGRAPHS   125

JUNGLE FEVER

GUESS WHO'S NOT COMING TO DINNER?   163
HENRY LOUIS GATES, JR.
PHOTOGRAPHS   170

CONTRIBUTORS   215

RIGHT ON, AS IN RIGHT ON TIME

HALLELUJAH—FIVE! (as in high five, as in give me five)—Our man Spike has a fifth feature under his belt! An African-American has five, bona fide, big-time, talking pictures, out there, with more to come!

FRANKLY, to tell the Truth, I was beginning to despair, then . . . all of a sudden—BAM!, it happened—and dere dey came charging up de hill! (Like my Grandmother used to say, referring to the Lord lending a helping hand with the rent, or a pair of new shoes, "HE may not come when you call HIM, but HE'S ALWAYS RIGHT ON TIME!")

Well, my grief was a little more abstract than rent, or shoes (and, thank-you-Jesus, a little premature). I was grieving over us African-Americans in the entertainment/communication media (especially filmmakingwise) not having any significant say in the way we were being portrayed, and not being able to project OUR OWN images of ourselves, OUR OWN interpretations of reality. (A crucial link in maintaining our heritage, and a key element to our present and future survival as a People.)

You see, about thirty-five years ago, circa 1955, I had had it with White Folks pushing their mythmaking machinery on us, running their bullshit from colonialism, to paternalism, to programmed genocide . . . after 400 years enough was ENOUGH. So I ate shit for the next fifteen years, including making two feature films, the first one—get this—as a French Director, thereby embarrassing Hollywood into finally giving a couple of Bloods a shot. (Up until then Hollywood had maintained that Jungle Bunnies weren't no way ready to be handling no stuff that complicated.)

Anyway, Jump cut to 1970. When I figured I was gonna finally change all that White Folks running the movie industry crap . . . my third feature, *SWEET SWEETBACK'S BAADASSSSS SONG* was ready to go! You see, I figured if I could just get *SWEETBACK* out there, overnight, IF NOT SOONER, Black Folks would be swarming all over the feature film business doing their thing.

Well, I pulled it off. I not only got the film into distribution, but it made a piss pot full of money. (Frankly I never expected *SWEETBACK* to become the financial success it became, that was an unexpected blessing . . . The Truth is I would have been deliriously happy just to break even and not getting my legs broken by disgruntled lenders. NOTE: I said LENDERS, not INVESTORS, because although I did manage to get some folks to LOAN me money, I couldn't get anyone to take an equity position in my harebrained scheme to make a movie where a nigger got away wid standing up to the Man.)

The profits that poured in, thanks to the uppity concept I introduced (BLACK HERO, NOT ONLY *SURVIVING BEYOND* THE FINAL FRAME OF THE PICTURE, BUT *ACTUALLY WINNING*), were not lost on Hollywood . . . No Sireee. Hollywood quickly adopted the concept, bringing out a tidal wave of Blaxploitation movies, along the way injecting a lethal political twist that defused my original message of self-determination, to a counter-revolutionary one by turning the hero into a tool (albeit a pseudo-maverick one), detective/undercover-agent/renegade-cop/extension of the Authorities, a.k.a. Bawana, a.k.a. the Status Quo, a.k.a. the Man Himself.

But the political implications of the scenario was only my FIRST grenade . . . I had

TWO! With the second grenade I wanted to blow up the idea that without his assistance we were helpless. What I was shooting for was to prove by example to Black Folks that we could do it completely by ourselves, without Massa's grants, approbations, or blessings. When the movie turned out to be a box office smash I felt that it was only a matter of seconds before a regiment of homeboys and girls would be storming up the hill to tear down the gates of Hollywood. I dug a foxhole and waited for reinforcement . . . I waited and waited . . .

Days, weeks, years rolled by . . . peeping over the rim of the trench I saw the majority of Black cinematographers denied the big prize of making feature films forced to ply less prestigious versions of the trade—shorts, documentaries, commercials, and videos. Occasionally (denied, or not) every now and then a lone African-American would come charging out of the forest with a finished feature tucked under his arm like a battering ram, heading up the hill for the gates to the Big-Time: Gordon Parks, Ossie Davis, Michael Schultz, Jamaa Fanaka, Sidney Poitier, Bill Greaves, St. Clair Bourne, Stan Lathan, Bill Gunn, and a few valiant others . . . but, Alas, by the time Homey reached the Hollywoodian gates, lacking a support system, he would be too exhausted to break down the door, or if successful in crashing the barrier would find himself being slowly preempted, allowed to make a film or two, then subtly touted by the racist system as the rule rather than the exception.

In the years after SWEETBACK there were less than 20 films actually controlled by African-Americans—That's what I was crouched in my hole grieving about . . . another DREAM DEFERRED. There I was . . . my canteen of FAITH bone-dry, my rations of HOPE long since gone, "Darky before the dawn," as they say, and all the rest, when . . . BAM!, like I mentioned before—what do I hear?

"TA-RA-TE-TA-TA-DAA!" a bugle blowing, CHAAARRGEEE! . . .

I sit up look around and there is this wave of African-American filmmakers barrelling up the hill (not a solitary filmmaker, easily picked off—NO, not this time). Here they come! . . . an endless row of young Black Filmmakers, charging up the road, stretching as far as the imagination can see and still growing, Directors like Robert Townsend, Keenen Ivory Wayans, Charles Burnett, my son Mario, Euzhan Palcy, Charles Lane, The Hudlin Brothers, etc. . . . Writers, Producers, Casting Directors, Lighting Directors, Editors, et al. . . . magnificent creatures, supportive towards one another, disciplined, clever, courageous, Wise to the ways of the Man, and Hip to the ways of the Street . . . and THERE leading the charge carrying the old banner of Self-Determination that Oscar Micheaux had stitched together so long ago, the Main-Man HIMSELF, Spike Lee.

WELL, like I said, HALLELUJAH. YES, Grandma was RIGHT, "HE may not come when you call HIM, but HE's ALWAYS RIGHT ON TIME!"

It is impossible to explain the thrill I experience when I see DIRECTED BY flashing across the screen with a Black name attached to it, or when I hear young Black filmmakers reply, when asked where-in-Heavens-name did they acquire the audacity to take on the system, mention me and SWEETBACK as their inspiration.

SPEAKING OF THRILLS, Spike has finished his fifth feature film, a momentous occasion if there ever was one. WELL, I would like to carve THANKS to him on his milestone from all African-Americans . . . and the rest of the world too (whether they know it or not, YET).

MELVIN VAN PEEBLES
December 1990

PREFACE

IS this my art? Not often enough, I would say if I were asked. I mean, of course it's my work, and I'm proud to be involved with all these films. I'm glad I'm Spike's brother, and not Steven Spielberg's—*Jaws* would've been tough since I can't swim, and I would've worked on *The Color Purple* only under protest, given the alterations from the book (and need we mention the added jubilee scene?).

I feel varying degrees of attachment, ranging from tolerance to a parent's embarrassing pride. The photo selection process (with me, Spike, and the able STC photo staff) was brutal but friendly, like a good pillow fight. I was pleased by the ground rules, which put no constraints on the pictures chosen. That is, they didn't necessarily have to be stills lifted "verbatim" from the films, burdened with faithfully recapping plots.

This being agreed upon, all hell broke loose, and with everybody's help I gained some and lost some good photos; but when the smoke cleared, I liked what I saw. My favorite shots, which I won't name, are those that surprise me, that appear almost out of context. It's some sleight of hand that by being relieved of any narrative duty, the photos are free to interpret Spike's work from a different, maybe unexpected angle. Discovery has always been my favorite component in my own or anyone else's work.

I suppose it could be argued that Spike is greater than any of his films, that synergism spiel about the whole being greater than the sum of its parts. It's my hope, then, that the stills presented here work on a parallel plane, that, at least occasionally, the photos are seen as something outside the films, and that they function as visual comments and addenda to the movies. If they're at times detached, all the better. Maybe I'm not a collaborator in Spike's film ventures, but being a contributor is more than fine, given the freedom that Spike has always allowed me.

A few last thoughts: I first have to give cinematographer Ernest Dickerson his due, since much of the set lighting was his. (Although now that I think about it, his lights were strategically placed to shoot their beam straight down the barrel of my lens, thus explaining the occasional flare.)

And finally, I shout out to my grandmother Mama and my brother Tone, whom, to my own astonishment, I recently referred to as the bookends of my life.

DAVID LEE
December 1990

FIVE FOR FIVE

SPIKE LEE

THE Jackson Five. The Five Satins. The Five Stairsteps. Five Fingers of Death. Joe DiMaggio, Johnny Bench, and Ed Charles—they wore the number five. My mother, Jacquelyn Shelton Lee, had five children. My brother's name is Cinque. The number five is a nice number. *She's Gotta Have It, School Daze, Do the Right Thing, Mo' Better Blues,* and the new joint *Jungle Fever*—that's 5 for 5. These five films have been produced over the last six years; with this productivity I felt it would be a good idea to take a quick pause for the cause and look back as we move ahead for the next five.

We've done four books, one for each film, with basically the same format. For *numero cinco* I wanted something different. I wanted this book to be a pictorial study of all my films. Cinema is a visual medium, and the books to date have been limited in their use of photos. My brother David Charles Lee, a gifted photographer (what else did you expect—he's a Lee), has been on the sets for each of my movies, and through his images, I hope the viewer sees the progression of the films and my craft.

I can't remember when my brother started to take pictures. He says he always did; I don't remember, or maybe I wasn't paying attention. When he went to Yale and studied photography, I realized he was serious about that camera, and this was fine by me. Right away I knew I would eventually recruit him to be the unit photographer on my films. His first assignment was the opening-credit sequence and winter montage in *She's Gotta Have It.* It's difficult for me to describe what it is about his work that I love. Yet I know I love it and the subjects he chooses. It doesn't take an art degree to see the growth in his photography, and this book showcases his talent.

One of the joys I've had being a filmmaker is including my family in the process. They've supported my work and benefited from it. My father, Bill Lee, has scored all my films up to *Mo' Better Blues;* he even did *Sarah* and *Joe's Bedstuy Barbershop: We Cut Heads,* two of my New York University student films. My sister, Joie, also has appeared in the first four, from *She's Gotta* to *Mo' Better.* In *Jungle Fever* neither participated. Joie felt it was time to start to establish her own identity (not only being Spike's sister). I felt the same way but offered her a small part, ya know, just to keep her working. She thought it better to refuse my offer, and she made the right choice. Now, with my father, it's another matter. We've done great work together; his scores keep getting better and better, but it was also getting harder for us to work together. So, we both mutually agreed to take a time-out. I hope we'll be able to come back together in the immediate future.

Because I work with my family, people believe we are close. Truth is, the films are the only things that bring us together. We don't stay in touch as much as we could and should. (This fact drives my grandmother, Zimmie Shelton, crazy: "Spike, how come you didn't know Cinque has been in Japan for a month? The rascal lives around the corner from you." I never have an answer; anyway, this is something all of us are trying to work on.) I feel that my brother's photography, my sister's acting, and my father's scores have not fully gotten the praise they deserve because of me. The perception is that David, Joie, and Daddy got the gigs because I'm their brother or I'm his son. But talent overruled everything else. My family worked with me because I felt they could do the job I needed done.

This attack also extends to attractive females I cast. So far, as rumor has it, I've cast Tracy Camila Johns, Rosie Perez, Cynda Williams, and Veronica Webb because I was attracted to them. Truth is, I've been attracted to a lot of women, but this won't get you in my movies. Being right for a particular role will.

Accompanying each film in this book is an essay by an impressive African-American writer. I long for the day when my films will be reviewed by a lot more African-American critics. Film isn't the only area that finds us lacking. Black artists in music, theater, dance, and other areas of the arts are ever so rarely given serious journalistic criticism by their own. So we got some people who can—and do—write their butts off from an African-American perspective: Melvin Van Peebles (the foreword), Terry McMillan (*She's Gotta Have It*), Toni Cade Bambara (*School Daze*), Nelson George (*Do the Right Thing*), Charles Johnson (*Mo' Better Blues*), and Dr. Henry Louis Gates (*Jungle Fever*). I'm a big fan of each of these writers' work, and I hooked them up with the film that I thought would best be served. I'm glad they all agreed to participate. The insight, vision, and criticism they express about my work are welcome.

To me, and also a lot of other young black filmmakers, Melvin Van Peebles is the man. We all know and read about pioneer filmmaker Oscar Micheaux. But Melvin did it in our lifetime, and he's alive to talk about what he did. His *Sweet Sweetback's Baadasssss Song* gave us the answers we needed. This was an example of how to make a film (a real movie), distribute it yourself, and most important, get *paid*. Without *Sweetback* who knows if there could have been a *Shaft* or *Superfly*? Or looking down the road a little further, would there have been a *She's Gotta Have It, Hollywood Shuffle,* or *House Party*? So it's fitting that Melvin do the foreword. He has witnessed in the last few years a rebirth of black filmmakers, and whether they know it or not, he has had a hand in their success.

To tell you the truth I hate talking about my work, but I'd rather tell my story than have somebody else do it. Growing up I wanted to be an athlete. The sport didn't matter; it just depended on what season it was: basketball, football, baseball, I played 'em all and still love 'em today. I had no idea that people made movies. I just didn't know. You went to the movie house, the lights went out, the movie came on, you enjoyed it, you ate as much popcorn and candy as you could eat, you drank as much Coke as you could drink, the movie ended, the lights came on, and you took your ass home. Movies were magic—and something you couldn't do. Or so you thought.

It's this perception of movies (which Hollywood promotes) that keeps folks from becoming filmmakers. We've been fed this hocus-pocus BS, so you think you can't do it. Film-making is a craft, and it can be learned like anything else; of course, it takes talent, but forget about it being something magical and mystical. There is a reason for that party line: Film is a powerful medium; it can influence how millions of people think, walk, talk, even live, plus you can make enormous sums of money. The idea is to keep the industry confined, let a small group of people have the control and make all the money. This is why one of my goals has been the demystification of film. I like to tell and show people it can be done. I'm saying don't fall for junk like, *You gotta be struck by lightning to be a filmmaker.* To this end, I hope that what I've written about my films has helped.

In sports there is always a critical moment, a turning point in the game; this moment determines whether you win or lose, not that everything up to that point didn't matter, but it's there that you have to pull through. I had a moment like that. I graduated from New York University Film School in 1982, and I was trying to do a feature film. I wrote this script called *Messenger;* it's about a bike messenger who has to become the head of his household when his mom dies of a heart attack. The project was overly ambitious, but I didn't know it at that time. In fact, I knew little about the real world of filmmaking; the NYU Film School stuff is a fantasy world. Anyway, in the summer of 1984, I tried to do this film. The producer was a friend of the family, and he promised he would raise the capital. I had known him a long time, and when he said he was gonna do something, I believed him. Well, *Messenger* was never shot, not one single frame of film. It was and still is the most painful experience in my professional life. We had hired a crew and cast the film; people were ready to go; we had everything, even had *Messenger* T-shirts. But what we didn't have was money. Every day my producer promised the money was coming. It never did.

We waited all summer. Finally, I had to pull the plug. I was getting physically ill; the project was making me sick: I couldn't sleep at night, and I couldn't eat because I would throw up. I've never weighed a lot to begin with, but I was surely one sickly, skinny melink. Everyone was let go: the film was off. We shut it down. I was devastated. My grandmother, Zimmie, who put me through college and film school, lost $20,000. Her money was gone. In total we lost about fifty grand; it could've been more than that. It was hard for me to face people; folks were mad as hell; and they had a right to be because they lost money and had turned down *real jobs, real employment,* to work on a nonexistent film. I was on everybody's shit list. One day, soon after the ship be sunk, I sat in a bathtub, filled with water, and cried— cried like a baby. I say this because I don't ever cry. I didn't even cry at my mother's funeral; I wanted to, but I felt I couldn't let my younger brothers and sister see me break down and do that. I had to be strong. Now, I'm not equating tears with weakness, but I believed at the time that because I was the eldest, my brothers and sister were looking to me for strength. I must have sat in that tub and cried for an hour. I was wrinkled as a raisin when I got out. I rehashed in my mind what happened, what I did wrong. I was a nice guy; why did this fucked-up shit have to happen to me? In retrospect, it happened to me for a reason: it made me stronger and more determined. This experience was my turning point. I had committed the cardinal sin of young filmmakers: I was in over my head. Everything—the budget, the size, the scope—was too big. *Joe's Bedstuy Barbershop: We Cut Heads* (my thesis film) was an hour-long student film. I swore on my mother's grave that I would never commit the errors I'd made on *Messenger* again and that next summer, the summer of 1985, I would be back. *We shall return.* I would write a script that was doable: use a few characters, no sets, funny dialogue, a little sex (well, maybe a lot). If I didn't have the money in the bank, I wouldn't shoot—no money, no production. Forget about it; I had learned my lesson. Well, maybe I hadn't learned it well enough, because when next summer rolled around, I had the script of *She's Gotta Have It* in hand but only $12,000 in the bank. We started work anyway. *She's Gotta* was shot in July 1985 in twelve days.

Of the five films I've done to date, this is the one I don't, can't, and refuse to watch. Why, you ask? It's because of the filmmaking and the performances. This film of mine is painful to me, so I don't watch it. You have to understand that when you see poor performances in a film, it's always the director's fault, for at least one of two reasons. Number one: He or she wasn't directing, so the actors were left alone to fend for themselves; actors need direction. Number two: The actors were miscast. I feel the director has to take the blame, and on *She's Gotta,* I was obviously still learning how to work with actors. I don't watch my films that much anyway. When a film comes out, I always go to the theaters in that first week or so of its release and watch it with the audiences. It's a good learning experience for me; I can tell exactly what works and what doesn't. If it works, it's great. Even though *She's Gotta* is not one of my favorites, it's because of that film that all else has been possible; so even though I can't watch it because of the pain I still feel, I'm grateful I made it. I had no idea the character of Mars Blackmon would take off the way it has. For me, Mars represented black youth, hip-hop; but he doesn't take or sell drugs or rape and mug people, ya know what I'm talkin' 'bout. He's funny.

When *She's Gotta* came out, I heard from Jim Riswald and Bill Davenport, who work at the advertising firm of Wieden and Kennedy. NIKE is their client. These two see the film, see Mars wearing Air Jordans, see Mars holding up Michael Jordan as his hero, and call me. We've been doing these commercials now for four years, and people still seem to like 'em (at least that's what they tell me); NIKE can't make enough of 'em. *Those young black kids must be really killing each other for those new Jordans.*

For me, one of the important things is that Michael Jordan and I hooked up. The bottom line is that two successful African-American men from different fields got together, met professionally, and created something. That's what is needed. I find it strange how I've done stuff with Michael Jordan, Denzel Washington, Mike Tyson, Jesse Jackson, and so on, but not with Eddie Murphy. And I'm not blaming Eddie either; it's both of our faults. We will hook up soon. Alliances like these are needed. Let's take note from those Lucas–Coppola jammies; white boys do it all the time.

It's because of the success of *She's Gotta* that the next film, *School Daze,* came about. Earlier, I had met David Puttnam, at that time the studio head at Columbia Pictures. He had liked *She's Gotta,* so when he called I was eager. I had met with a lot of studio people; one person I recall is Sean Daniels, who was then at Universal. He said no to *School Daze* (he was later instrumental in bringing *Do the Right Thing* there). *Daze* was a real movie; *She's Gotta* had been made mostly with friends and relatives and $175,000. *Daze* was 6.5 million bucks. Now, I know a lot of people felt that was too big a jump for a novice filmmaker. I didn't feel that way, so it didn't matter.

Being a third-generation Morehouse man I wanted to do a film on the unique black college experience. In fact, I jammed my four years of college into a two-hour movie. This probably accounts for the one criticism I always hear, "Too much is happening." All I can say is that was my intent. I don't want to or can't say which film is my favorite. You could say it's like asking parents who their favorite child is; they might have one, but they'll never say. What I liked about *Daze* was the musical numbers: "Straight and Nappy," "Be One," "Be Alone Tonight," and "Da Butt," which became a number-one hit record and a national dance craze. The critical reaction to *Daze* was another thing altogether. On *She's Gotta,* we gathered mostly glowing reviews, but the next time around, this was not the case. Critics like to build you up, tear you down, and then, if you're lucky, build you up again. The criticism from black folks hit us the hardest. One *Amsterdam News* reviewer said *Daze* put the black race back two hundred years. People objected to airing dirty laundry—in this case meaning my portraying the prejudices we black people have among ourselves based on skin complexion, hair texture, etc. For me, it was not a big secret; we've always had these prejudices (at least since Massa started to sneak into the slaves' quarters and dilute our blood), and they are still present today. I myself considered the film a success; we touched on new ground, and I was learning my craft, the most important point. This whole filmmaking business is a process. The dance scene in *She's Gotta* helped me form the musical numbers in *Daze*. The big scenes in *Daze* prepared me for doing the riot in *Do the Right Thing*. The bigger scope in *Right Thing* only made *Mo' Better Blues* that much easier.

I won't say much about *Right Thing*. The Howard Beach incident inspired me to do the movie, and we just went on from there. What people don't know is that the first day the film opened, I was in front of the National Theatre on Broadway. A huge crowd was around me, and I was signing autographs. Standing next to me were two cops, who were trying to keep me from being crushed. Well, someone called the cops and reported that black people were attacking cops in front of the theater. Six police cars came screeching down Broadway, sirens blaring. The cops jumped out with guns and billy clubs drawn. This was just like a scene from the movie. I remember this one cop, his face was beet red, veins popping from his neck. He started yelling at me, and I started yelling back—to which the crowd started cheering. Then it hit me like a ton of bricks: this could be the start of some serious shit. I could see the headlines: *Spike Lee's* Do the Right Thing *Starts Riot in Times Square*.

This is exactly what some writers like Joe Klein and David Denby of *New York* magazine and Jack Kroll of *Newsweek* were predicting. I stopped and smiled at the cop; the whole thing was diffused. You have never seen someone so disappointed. This policeman had a great opportunity to crack some niggers' heads, and it didn't pan out. I just felt sorry for the next brother who was gonna get it. For me, this film was a litmus test: You could actually tell which critics were closet redneck racist peckerwoods. That whole litany about whether Mookie did or didn't do the right thing was a joke. Some of these critics were more concerned about Sal's Pizzeria burning down than they were with a human life—a black human life. But then again, maybe they didn't consider Radio Raheem human but had neatly relegated him to subhuman, a wilding animal—*exactly like all young black males are. Radio Raheem is the same as those kids Bernard Goetz shot and maimed. Radio Raheem is the same as those black bastards who raped that white woman in Central Park. Radio Raheem is the same as all these animals who drop out of high school, rob, steal, murder, father unwanted babies, and use and sell crack.* So, of course, the racist critics would be more concerned about the destruction of private property, Sal's Pizzeria, in that ghetto, Bedford-Stuyvesant. *Radio Raheem isn't human; he's an animal with a ghetto blaster, polluting the environment with that rap noise "Fight the Power."*

Regardless, we rode way above the critics' garbage and went straight into *Mo' Better Blues*. I kinda figured the critics would be laying for me once again; they just had to wait to see what the focus would be. Well, on *Mo' Better*, the word was that Spike Lee was an anti-Semite; Moe and Josh Flatbush were stereotypes. *Spike*, the critics asked, *how could you do this; don't you know your history? Jews marched alongside King. How can you portray us in this light?* The gibes continued: *Spike, there has never been a crooked Jewish manager, club owner, record label owner, studio head who has ever exploited black artists; we love black people. You've been, the blacks have been, persecuted almost as much as we have. Spike, we're the chosen people. You better stop hanging out with Jesse Jackson; now that's a real anti-Semite.* Well, I have to give it to my Jewish brothers and sisters: there may be only seven million of them here in America, but they can lobby like motherfuckers. Say something they feel is anti-Semitic or against the state of Israel and you'll know about it *right away*.

Now, I'm not gonna take this space to defend myself again, which I did already in the *New York Times* (Op Ed page, August 22, 1990, page 19), and I shouldn't have to anyway, but that's something African-Americans need to pick up from Jews. We let other people get away with murder; we don't say or do nuthin', no letters, no postcards, no telegrams, no phone calls, no boycotts, no nuthin', but let someone say something or write about Jews that they don't like, and all hell breaks loose. To this day, I don't know what causes the upset when it's stated that for the most part people of Jewish ancestry run the entertainment industry. This is not an indictment, and it's not a moral judgment. It's like saying the National Basketball Association is made up mostly of African-Americans. I've made three films at Universal Pictures, and I know that the people who run things are Lew Wasserman, Sidney Sheinberg, Tom Pollack, Fred Bernstein, and Sy Kornblitt. And the sale of MCA to the Japanese doesn't negate this. I also find it amazing that *Mo' Better* prompted journalists and film critics who have been writing for years and have seen thousands of movies to write articles about stereotypes in movies for the first time. WHAT THE FUCK IS THAT? It took a film by a black filmmaker to bring this on? That's a joke. Gene Siskel and Roger Ebert (who I admit are two of my biggest supporters) have been on TV for years and never before did a show on stereotypical images. Then *Mo' Better* comes out, and they devote a full show to this topic. What about all those other films, where blacks, gays, and women are getting dogged left and right? I guess that doesn't count; it only matters when a black filmmaker does it. I'm gonna say this, and I'll continue to say it until things change. This good ole U.S. of A. has two motherfucking standards and sets of rules: one white and one black.

To black folks, I say let's make up our own rules. As I'm writing this, we're working around the clock 24, 7 trying to complete the fifth film, *Jungle Fever*. We had fireworks on *Do the Right Thing*, but I feel they are small compared to the fallout that will come after this new one. *Do the Right Thing* was about race and class, but *Jungle Fever* combines those two, plus sex, and this makes a much more combustible combination. You have two extremes: a young married African-American architect who lives on Striver's Row in Harlem and a young Italian-American woman, a temp secretary from Bensonhurst. Put these two together, and somebody is gonna die. In August 1989, Yusuf Hawkins got on a train to look at a used car; he was headed to Bensonhurst. We all know what happened. In my eyes, he was lynched. Yusuf Hawkins is Emmet Till. Both were murdered for alleged reckless eyeballing. As I write this piece, one by one, the defendants in the Bensonhurst case walk scot-free. It's a crime, and Yusuf and Bensonhurst were definitely on my mind when I wrote this script. I made a point of shooting in that neighborhood. One night we received three bomb threats. Wes Snipes, who played the architect, and I got a rock thrown at us. Ernest Dickerson, our cameraman, got hit by a rock. The New York *Daily News* had me on the front page with headlines screaming "Cops Guard Spike Lee" (September 21, 1990), and the set that night was a real circus of reporters and TV crews; it was mayhem. Looking back, we were well received in the Brooklyn neighborhoods of Mill Basin and Bensonhurst, despite those rock-missile incidents. Going in, I thought it was gonna be much worse. Of course, when *Jungle Fever* comes out, I may want to change what I just wrote.

Having done five films in six years, I know for sure I cannot keep up this pace; it could kill me. The reason for this pace is simple: historically, black filmmakers have found it extremely hard to go from film to film. I didn't want a long layoff between films. When things are clicking, ya gotta stay with it. So many of our stories are yet to be told, and I am getting a shot to tell the ones I know in films. Cinema is the most important thing in my life, and I've been given unique opportunities to have full creative control on films that I want to make. I can't turn that down. That's why we've been working like a Georgia mule "from can't see in the morning to can't see at night" the past six years. But Woody Allen has a faster pace, and he's twenty years older than me, and it hasn't killed him yet. All that we have done at Forty Acres and a Mule has prepared us for our next film, certain to be our biggest yet and the most important—*Malcolm X.*

I could fill ten books like this with names of people who have helped me make my way. I'd like to thank everyone, and especially Monty Ross, Ernest Dickerson, Bill Lee, and my grandmother—they've been with me from the git-go.

SHE'S GOTTA HAVE IT

THOUGHTS ON SHE'S GOTTA HAVE IT

TERRY McMILLAN

1986: IN RETROSPECT

THE title alone was alluring. She's gotta have what? According to folks who'd already seen Spike Lee's first feature film, "she" had to have exactly what I was almost afraid she had to have: sex. Could a filmmaker be this bold and just come right on out and say it? Well, Spike Lee had already said it: *She's Gotta Have It.* My first clue that this was a *real* and up-to-the-minute black film was the use of *gotta.* Some of us—African-American women and men—try hard to avoid the use of this kind of slang once we've achieved a certain educational status, but not Spike Lee, a Brooklynite who I knew had a master's degree from New York University. I welcomed the street quality, which is another way of saying he was still down (not stiff or formal) or hadn't-forgotten-where-he-came-from yet. Let's face it. Some of us haven't realized that you can be both educated and not ashamed of using our own jargon. Because *no* one else talks like us, the use of *gotta* in the title was a signal to me of the kind of language that would be used in the film. To me, such use did not imply that the characters would be illiterate or inarticulate but that they would be regular people. This pleased me. I would've had an altogether different feeling had the title been, say, *She Must Have It* or even *She's Got to Have It.* Neither would have had anywhere near *She's Gotta*'s deliberate aggressiveness and, I'd go so far as to say, crudeness. But sometimes, that's what you have to do to grab folks' attention. It worked on me, so, now, let's see how much she's gotta have.

A few friends (black and white alike) who purported to be film buffs and who were self-ordained critics, hence, the Vincent Canbys and Pauline Kaels of the Upper West Side and Brooklyn, had already given me part of the lowdown on the film: it was "stylized; it was sort of like those old French *film noir* movies [I had forgotten what that meant at the time]; the structure was ingenious; he employed the documentary form called cinema verité [which I did remember!]—now updated and transformed into a fictive plot; and [last but not least], *it put you in mind of the works of Woody Allen, in some ways* [italics added]." My friends tried hard to sound highly intellectual and original, but their often nonsensical comments were a repeat of what they'd already read in the newspaper or heard on Siskel and Ebert's *Sneak Preview.* Sometimes I had to cover the phone to stop them from hearing me laugh. Of course, these were the same folks who saw almost every foreign film on 58th Street, saw revivals at the old Thalia on 95th Street, or sat at parties trying to dissect, translate, and elucidate what they'd seen and trying even harder to impose value judgments on a genre when none was often even necessary. Nevertheless, my initial question had been a generic one, and virtually the same: "Did you like it?"

"Well, yes," they all echoed.

Anyway, one such person called and was ready to reveal the entire story line. "Don't say another word about it," I demanded. "I'm going to see it tomorrow." I could, however, tell by individual testimonies and the *desire* to testify what each person had experienced—something poignant, funny, and what was apparently a realistic and contemporary portrayal of us. According to one person, this film was "some kind of tour de force" of the cinema. "All I can say is, it's definitely a black thang."

I liked that. Which meant that the narrative was probably whimsical and had a beat and rhythm to it that we clearly could relate to; that the language hadn't been manipulated so that it didn't sound like us; and that the nuances, idiosyncrasies, mannerisms, and perhaps the story itself were something so closely akin to our everyday experiences that white folks would probably have to see it two or three times to understand certain things or have to ask somebody black what certain things meant. I've had this happen with my own work.

Being a nosy person, I did ask a few questions so I would know up front what I might be in for. "Just tell me this," I said. "It's not anything close to those blaxploitation films of the '70s, is it?" My fingers were crossed.

"Hell no," one said. "It's definitely different from that mess, but I don't exactly know how to classify it."

"How does he treat women?" I asked.

"I thought you didn't want me to tell you any more."

"Okay, then stop," I said. She didn't sound pissed off, so I assumed Spike Lee's portrayal of black women was realistic, sympathetic, or at least three-dimensional.

"Wait," I said, "just tell me *one* more thing. She's not a nympho, is she?"

"I'm not saying," my friend said, laughing. "But it's deep." Then she hung up.

Even though I was burning up on the No. 4 train, I was excited as all get out. I get that way when I'm going to see a movie I've already heard rumors about. But this was a different kind of excitement. I was thinking that this *brother* was young—younger than any other filmmaker I'd heard of—and that this was his first feature film. I'd already heard that he had to beg, borrow, and damn-near steal to come up with the $175,000 to get it made. This made me and a whole lot of other folks mad. How can you make a decent movie on a shoestring budget? Then I thought about all the recent Hollywood megamovies that ran from six to eight figures. I acquired instant admiration for this young man; I admired his verve, his belief in his work, and especially his determination to get his vision on the screen. Not enough of us out here stick our necks out this far, trust our own creative decisions with respect to our particular craft, or have the desire and will to use extraordinary means to get something we believe in accomplished. I know too many folks who aren't willing to sacrifice or give up anything but who want it *all*. Now.

Somebody had mentioned that *She's Gotta Have It* was both funny and serious. How would Spike Lee accomplish both? I wondered, as the train jutted along the East Side. How will he tell his story? No one had really told me what the *story* itself was about with the exception of, "It's about a sister with a serious sex jones . . . ," and "this sister is dealing with three men, girl, three!" or "It's a trip."

Would it be structured like a novel, stockpiling everything? Would it be slow, from a whisper to a scream or the other way around? What if it's corny? Tacky? Sleazy?

I'd seen the ad, which I thought was comical, and a *She's Gotta Have It* T-shirt, which I coveted because the sister who was apparently the star was definitely sensuous, wearing that hot-pink lipstick with her mouth open in laughter and those hot-pink fingernails spread across her chest. I wanted to know where the people I'd seen on the train and on the streets had found the T-shirts, especially when I saw that "Please baby, please baby, please baby, baby baby please" on the back. I cracked up. Somebody was begging for it! And thank God she wasn't your typical Hollywood pretty (didn't look like a high-fashion model), wasn't high yellow and skinny as a rail, and didn't have long flowing hair!

I had never heard of any of the actors before. The star syndrome does get old, so I saw this move as a smart one *if* these folks could act. Then, I started thinking about how anxious and excited *some* black actors become when they finally procure a role of any magnitude and get paid: a lot of them overact. I hoped that this wouldn't be the case. If the *story* is good (and I prayed there *was* one because I'd seen enough meaningless films to last a lifetime), then perhaps the use of inexperienced actors was not so much a shortcut to save money but to do what's rarely done in Hollywood: Give black actors with talent a chance. If they are believable, use authentic speech, and don't look or sound as if they are acting per se, then I am in for a treat.

But what if the story is dreadful? What if this young filmmaker rips black women to shreds? That's what some black men say that black female writers do to them. Will this be the beginning of payback? And will I take it personally? No, I thought, as I ran up the steps at 34th Street. If this film attacks black women, I can't possibly take it personally because I don't know this Spike Lee person. Maybe he'd met some brutal, insensitive, selfish, calculating women in his short lifetime, enough so that it motivated him to examine these types of relationships in film. Hell, he had a right to express his feelings any way he wanted to. I called it freedom of expression; it's in the Constitution.

I walked four blocks to my friend's building, staring into those East Side boutique windows at items I couldn't afford but coveted. I hoped there was more to the main character in this movie than her shrinking or unsatiated libido. Because if there wasn't, then this was going to be a flat, homogenized, one-dimensional movie. Something told me that because this was the brother's first time out, it had to break through more than just the surface.

I had refused to read any reviews, especially those in *The New York Times, Time* magazine, and *Newsweek* magazine. And I presumed that the review in *Vanity Fair* would eventually add its normal nonmagnanimous hyperbole. I don't trust white critics' judgment about most things that deal with black life, particularly when a black person is the creator. It never fails. White critics always seem to misinterpret *us* because they don't understand *us* (or don't care to), so I wasn't alarmed when I started hearing the repetitious echoes of Spike Lee being compared to Woody Allen. It's no secret that as soon as any black artist does something remotely unique, he or she is compared to a white (in this case Jewish) artist. (The antithesis of this, however, is that black artists are constantly being compared to each other, usually for one reason: because we're black.)

It was hot as hell by now. It was Sunday afternoon, and my girlfriend and I had caught a cab from her apartment to the Cinema Studio (the only theater where the film was playing in Manhattan) on Broadway, right across the street from Lincoln Center. About fifty or so folks were in line, but it didn't take long before at least a hundred more were behind us. Lord knows I hate standing in line to see any film, especially in the summer heat and humidity in New York City, but it had already cost me $4.00 to get here, so we decided to get a soda and wait in line patiently with the rest of the growing crowd.

What was immediately refreshing was seeing so many black folks standing out in the sweltering sun to see a film by a black filmmaker. It was as if we were all hungry for almost any image we could find of ourselves, if even in the end we only criticized it. How long had it been since we'd seen a nonsentimental, humorous (not parodic), decent, and exciting portrayal of *us* in a film? At the time, I couldn't remember. While my girlfriend and I stood in line, looking around to see how many fine men were behind and in front of us, we saw this guy with a baseball cap walking from the back of the line toward us. He was passing out something that looked like a button, and he was shaking hands and saying thank you. Spike Lee? It certainly was. I tapped my girlfriend on the arm. "Girl, Spike Lee is passing out buttons for his movie! Can you believe it?" She just looked at me and said, "Y'all got something in common then, girl." What she meant was, I had spent six months developing and implementing my own private PR campaign for my first novel because I couldn't count on my publisher to do it. They flat out refused to spend any money to promote it—so I understood precisely why Spike Lee was handing out buttons. If you want to make sure something gets done, you have to do it yourself.

As I watched him come toward us, I started thinking. Did John Huston ever have to do this? D. W. Griffith? Fellini? Woody Allen? Robert Altman? Martin Scorsese? I doubted it. It's still about Forty Acres and a Mule.

One aspect of this film that I'd heard about caused me the most worry: It was in black and white. This wasn't exactly a turn-on for me because I had a reputation for falling asleep during black-and-white films in college. No one had said that the film's lack of the use of color didn't work or that it worked against the film. I'd read in the accompanying book to *She's Gotta Have It* (*Spike Lee's Gotta Have It,* New York: Simon & Schuster, 1986) that Spike wanted the film to have the texture and look of the French *film noir* movies of the 1940s and 1950s, and to achieve this effect, it could only be done in black and white. I wondered if he would've shot it in color if he'd had more money.

Finally, the line started moving. We got good seats, right in the middle. I ran back out and got our popcorn and Coke. While standing in line, I heard a few folks say, "This is my third time seeing it." Others dittoed. I smiled, went and sat back down, and waited. Now a humming was in the room that sounded almost like a chant or a mantra, and I could feel the anticipation and excitement in the entire theater. Some people were already laughing. My cheeks were hurting from the grin I was holding inside because I didn't even know what was funny.

The lights went low. The previews were too damn long. The screen went black. Then the curtains closed and reopened. (If I'm remembering right, but if there weren't any curtains, so what. The point is, I was anxious.) A square white light projected onto the screen and then it went black again. That's when I heard the music. The tone of the score alone surprised me because I was expecting some hip-hop music (don't ask me why) or something loud and boisterous, but this music reminded me of a bluesier, quieter version of Scott Joplin and then like a jazz piano, but it could've been a harpsichord. Then it sounded blue.

Seconds later, I started reading what I knew to be the opening of *Their Eyes Were Watching God,* a novel by Zora Neale Hurston. I elbowed my girlfriend. "*He* knows who Zora Neale is, girl!" Then I leaned back in my seat and read the following:

Ships at a distance have every man's wish on board. For some they come in with the tide. For others they sail forever on the horizon, never out of sight, never landing until the Watcher turns his eyes away in resignation, his dreams mocked to death by Time. That is the life of men. Now, women forget all those things they don't want to remember, and remember everything they don't want to forget. The dream is the truth. Then they act and do things accordingly.

Tell it, Zora! She'd said it right, and she'd said it first. Now Spike Lee was letting the world at large read and see a small yet significant sample of her vision. And for those who'd never heard of Hurston (there are still millions), maybe the passage would arouse their curiosity enough to go out and discover her works.

Okay. I might as well admit it now. I too am one of those pseudo-film buffs I dissed earlier who thinks she has a few inside clues as to the what, how, and why a filmmaker is doing what he or she has chosen to do in a particular way. So, what follows is perhaps what could best be described as not only educated guesses but my subjective reactions to this film. I've never had to provide my opinion of any film that I knew would appear in print, so please bear with me. So far, I'm having fun.

I leaned back in my seat and stuffed a handful of popcorn in my mouth while the first credit filled the screen: Forty Acres and a Mule Filmworks. What a name for a film company, I thought. Undoubtedly appropriate because I was sure it meant to connote just how hard it is to get a film made, especially by Hollywood standards. And most likely, how hard it would continue to be. Then I saw "A Spike Lee Joint" and prayed he didn't mean the kind of joint many of us were familiar with. But the word *joint*—at least where I come from—has a few definitions: (1) a prison; (2) a place—any place, really, as in your house (aka crib) or your apartment; (3) cool or happening, the place to be, as in "It was the joint, man!" and (4) a party. I decided that "A Spike Lee Joint" was a combination of 2, 3, and 4.

Anyway, after the title rolled down on the screen in lowercase letters, that made me think that this movie was definitely going to be down and that Spike Lee was about to break some rules.

I waited for motion, but the next thing I saw was a black-and-white photograph that looked like it was taken in the 1950s or 1960s. The photo was of a kid standing in front of some graffiti on a brick building that said something about some folks in Bed-Stuy should consider forming another republic, separate from the USA. I cracked up and started nodding my head. Before I could think about whether I'd ever seen a film that used a still photograph in its opening, more came, all with the same nostalgic look to them.

Then the credits for the actors appeared. Tracy Camila Johns's name was first. I took a sip of my soda and started thinking about when was the last time a black actress had a leading role in any film? I said a silent thank you to Spike Lee for that alone. Like I said earlier, I didn't recognize a single name, so I was curious as to who would be who and what relationship they would each have to the leading lady.

More black-and-white photographs: a little boy trying to drag another little brother in a direction he didn't want to go; a street scene of a black neighborhood, which indicated to me that this film was not going to be about uppity black folks or any Hollywood, superficial bullshit; little boys and girls innocently holding hands in a half circle, conscious only of the person taking their picture; a boy pumping high on a swing; various shots of black men in black leather caps, plaid shirts, and car coats; and a lonely black man in an old Stetson. An old white man holding something in one of these photographs was a signal to me that most likely, whites weren't going to be in this movie, or if they were, their roles wouldn't be crucial ones (for a change).

It took me a second to realize there was movement in the last of these stills. I saw shadows and silhouettes of people walking behind gridirons of some kind and then noticed what appeared to be a suspension bridge. The lens was still when it focused on the cables, which, of course, were crisscrossing. And when the camera panned their length, I said, "Yep, this is about entanglement of some kind." And besides, a bridge leads to somewhere else, it connects you to something. As the camera left the bridge and focused on a warehouse, I knew this was the place it might all happen.

I wasn't prepared, however, for the next movement. Someone was moving under the covers in a bed! What a way to start! Doing it. The fluid and smooth movement gave me a clue that these people were at least making love and not engaging in hard-core fucking. I was shocked when this black woman sat up in slow motion and looked directly at the camera and then her name appeared on the screen: Nola Darling. I liked this shit already. This was a new one on me. Her name itself had a touch of innocence (I thought about the Little Rascals; wasn't there a Darla in Our Gang?) Then Nola started talking to me. "I want you to know the only reason I consented to this is because I want to clear my name . . ." At first, I just thought she was an attractive sister, but by the time she finished telling me the deal, she was sexy and sensuous and became beautiful because she seemed to know exactly who she was. I was thrilled. I mean, I remember watching tons of documentaries in which the person talked directly to the camera, providing you with factual information that would accompany the visuals. One rarely sees this method used in movies today, a method that is part of cinema verité and that Spike was using differently. I liked it. So far.

And those candles around the bed. It was kind of scary to me, like this was a bewitching bed instead of a "loving bed." What also became apparent immediately was that Spike Lee had started his story at the end. When she said, "Some people call me a freak," I shoved some more popcorn in my mouth and sat straight up. I knew that the shit hadn't worked out, whatever it was, so now, let me find out how and why. I leaned back in my seat.

When we meet Jamie Overstreet (Tommy Redmond Hicks), he is sitting on a park bench, whistling and reading a paper. He (player 1) looks at *me* in complete earnest and says, "I believe that there is only one person, only one in this world that is meant to be your soul mate, your lifelong companion." Although he had a great baritone voice, I knew right off the bat that Jamie was the father-figure type; he was entirely too damn serious and looked too intense (almost scary), like he knew exactly what he wanted and wasn't going to be satisfied until he got it. He seemed like the type of man who would try to put the clamps on you after you fucked him real good and then you wouldn't be able to get rid of him. This type of man can really get on your nerves. He also struck me as the type who rarely laughed; who would orchestrate and plan out your entire life, once you married him; who would decide for you when he thought it was time to have the kiddies and where and what kind of house you lived in; and who would try to stop you from doing, once he married you, the very same "wild" things that initially attracted him to you. He'd drag your ass to the suburbs and try to keep you from your friends and anybody you knew in your other life that could possibly have more influence over you than he did. I was not at all crazy about Jamie from jump street.

When Jamie gets to Nola's loft and I see the ritualistic manner in which she lights what seems like hundreds of candles around her bed, I'm thinking that old Jamie isn't the only one with whom she's doing this. So when they're doing the "wild thing" and she tells him she loves him, I know she's lying. I know the sex is good, and it's clear that he's tickled that she has said it and that he actually believes her. What an idiot.

Now. Making love was just beautiful in slow motion. I'd *never* seen a real black couple in the twentieth century on screen making love before, nor had I ever seen a black woman actually *enjoying* it! It's about damn time! And when Nola licked her tongue out in obvious glee, even though we didn't actually see them "doing it" (only a hint of her breasts was revealed), the facial expressions and the music alone told me how wonderful this was for them both. All I remember thinking—tinged, of course, with a little nostalgic envy—was that Nola knew what she wanted and she got it. What a new twist. When those candles burned out, I knew they were finished, but when he asked her what could he do for her, I was almost in shock. I elbowed my girlfriend. "When was the last time some man asked you that afterwards?" She just shook her head and said, "Girl, I can't remember, ever." So Jamie wasn't a selfish lay. He cared about old Nola, and when she told him that most men she's dealt with don't know a thing about a woman's body, the whole theater said aloud, "Amen," and "I wanna thank you!" It's the truth, but I don't even want to get into it here.

The weird part was when she told him that she could only do "it" in her bed. The only thing that made any sense to me was that she had to have it the way she wanted it, where she wanted it, and on her own terms. It was as if this whole candle business and her bed, which was prominently placed in the middle of the huge loft, were her own fantasies that she had to live out. That old Jamie went along with this program told me not only how good her stuff was but how much he wanted to be with her. What a fool, I thought. He wants her too bad.

So next we meet an old friend of Nola's: Clorinda Bradford (Joie Lee), an ex-roommate who still seems a bit peeved at Nola's comings and goings and all the men she used to have in their apartment. But apparently she still cares about her friend Nola; they just don't stay in touch anymore.

When we get back to Nola and she says—and Lord knows I love this quote—"I've found two types of men: the decent ones and the dogs," then we meet and hear fifteen of them with a host of tacky lines women have been getting for years. Spike punctuates the end of this sequence with the sound of real barking dogs. My cheeks were hurting from laughing so hard. Some of the things they say are just "weak," as Nola put it. But try telling them that. Spike Lee was working this from the inside, and I appreciated that.

Then we meet Mars Blackmon (Spike Lee), and here again the name implies that he's perhaps a little out there (spaced), and, of course, he's a "blackman" (in Brooklyn you hear a lot of West Indians say "mon" as man). He's clearly young (early to mid-twenties), wearing those Cazal designer glasses all the young boys in Manhattan and Brooklyn were wearing then.

The camera is so close to Mars's face that he looks like some kind of a freak. When Mars says, "I thought she was a freak," I could tell he didn't really mean it. What Nola had probably done was blow his young mind. Mars is obviously player 2, and I was curious as to how he was going to pursue Ms. Darling. I couldn't believe it when he actually came right out and admitted that "all men want freaks, we just don't want 'em for a wife." "I know," I said aloud. "Thank you for telling the truth!"

Mars is a smart, wisecracking, funny young man who doesn't seem to take himself seriously but definitely knows how much he craves Nola Darling's body. I think he wants to grow up and be treated like a man (people apparently don't take him seriously). When he meets her and comes into her place checking it out and when he can't believe the whole place is hers, I saw an opportunist for a minute but then realized he wasn't about that. He is impressed, as if he has never dealt with this "kind" of woman (someone with a job, her own place, and so forth). Kiddingly, he asks her whether she needs a roommate, but Nola takes him seriously. Tells him point-blank in the form of a rhetorical question that why is it that every man she brings up here, the next thing they want to do is move in? I was surprised when Mars tells her that he pays his own way and that he doesn't like leeches either. Introductions are finished, the ice is broken, and they're both clear on a few things now. But now what are they going to do with each other? I wondered. I'll tell you right now that I'd have taken Mars over Jamie because Jamie had no character at all. Mars was a character, which in and of itself made him more interesting to me. But I guess the question that concerned Nola, as well as me (and other people in the audience), was this: Could Mars do the wild thing as good as Jamie? We'd find out soon enough, I supposed.

I was waiting for player 3. In the meantime, here comes the lesbian, Opal Gilstrap (Raye Dowell). My first cause of alarm was that *Jamie* tells us about Opal. In addition, he is fully aware that Nola has other male "friends." I found this hard to accept, but then again . . .

Opal obviously poses a threat to Jamie, which told me how insecure he was in general and also how shaky his shit was with Nola. He is vying for first place, and his competition is both men and women. How many black men would actually tolerate this kind of "division" in a relationship with a black woman? But this was a movie, which should, in some situations, be overexaggerated and drawn a bit out of proportion to make a point. I took this to be one of those kinds of situations.

Opal looks at the camera as if she is trying to seduce it (like Marilyn Monroe used to do) until she starts talking and tells us what she is. I didn't trust her from jump street, even when she tells us that Nola is "straight as an arrow" but she wants her to be open-minded.

Opal tries to gussy up to Nola when she's sick in bed with a cold, and Nola asks Opal what it's like making love to a woman. I was curious because Nola was curious, and thought, what better person to ask? When Opal expresses how appalled she is by men and the way she describes what it's not, "some musty man pounding away inside you a mile a minute," I cracked up but felt the disgust myself for a minute until I started thinking about the men who didn't do it that way.

When Jamie arrives and all three of them are in the room, somehow we know they've met before and it's a territorial thing they're dealing with, and *Nola* is the territory. It was funny, watching them both sit it out the way young men used to do when they'd come to visit when I wasn't old enough to date and my mama and daddy would act like they were never going to get sleepy and go to bed. They'd sit there and wait to make sure neither one of us had to go to the bathroom. At the same time!

Spike played this scene up; I wondered, in real life would this really be plausible? What kind of man and how many men would've even put themselves in such a ridiculous situation? Then I realized that some men would put themselves in this position and wouldn't be satisfied until they won. This was about Jamie's ego, his manhood.

When this fine black man who reminded me of Billy Dee Williams pulls through a gated driveway in a convertible Jaguar, takes off his shades, looks arrogantly into the camera and swings his slicked-back wavy-haired head back and then forward, and says, "I was the best thing that ever happened to Nola Darling," I knew that he was player 3 and was an asshole. He was a pretty boy, a superficial one that I figured was a transplant from LA. But why isn't he driving a BMW? "Nola was rough when I started seeing her," he said. "A Brooklyn tack-head. But I refined her." Give me a fucking break! Oh, oh, I thought, this one is going to try to mold her into his own little movable statue so that she would be his very own work of art. He even said that she was but a mere "lump of clay" until she met him! Greer Childs (John Canada Terrell) clearly detests Brooklyn and thinks it's a lower-class borough. If he wasn't from LA, then it meant he probably lives on the Upper East Side in a high rise. What he did for a living, I couldn't tell immediately.

Okay. So these are all the players. And by the time I finished watching how they "played" for the next eighty-or-so minutes, I was often shocked and bowled over in laughter, yet I took Nola Darling's dilemma seriously.

To me, the story was about power: exercising power over your own body and mind. In this case, it was a black woman. What a switch. I mean, Hollywood is notorious for having males in leading roles with some kind of outside love "interests." And even when a male character is dealing with more than one woman, he is never referred to or viewed as a freak but as a sexually imaginative, sexually active, or sexually aggressive man. Men in general have gone through their little black books on Friday nights and gone through the entire alphabet until they can get a woman to come over (Mars even does it after he calls Nola and she turns him down), and have been known to boast about having ménage à trois. They are also good at planning many of their seductions well in advance. It was refreshing to see a black woman doing the same thing.

So what Spike Lee has done is give viewers not only a female version of male sexual mores but a main character who is still very much a woman. We have Nola Darling, a young black woman who doesn't sit by the phone waiting for a man to call; she asserts herself and comes right out and tells each man that if he wants to play, then he has to play by her rules. This is the way it is or should have been in the 1980s. That a black male filmmaker chose to illustrate and tell the story from a female perspective made me feel great. How many black women are like Nola Darling? Not enough. Millions have never had an orgasm and still wait to be approached by men.

Not once does Nola say she wants a husband or even a long-term boyfriend. She only repents when Jamie gives her an ultimatum—choose him over the other two men in her life—with the threat of leaving her if she refuses. Nola seems only to feel insecure about not having him in her little black book anymore, so she acquiesces—lies to him and herself—by telling him, begrudgingly and with much contemplation, that he's the one she has chosen.

The other thing that fascinated me was how Spike Lee managed to show how wimpy men can be when it comes to a woman. They can be just as stupid as we can, although women have traditionally been shown as vulnerable and weak. I kept wondering throughout the film if it was just that Nola had pussy-whipped them all into submission or if some other redeeming quality to her personality made them act like possessed fools.

It seemed as if Spike Lee tried to show us something about the male ego as well— the need to always be on top (literally and figuratively). The prize was a woman, and although the three men, especially Jamie, resented being controlled by Nola, each fervently struggled to win her.

I'm not so sure whether Nola ever took Mars seriously (I don't think he ever believed he was even a real contender). I do think, however, that Nola was only attracted to Greer initially because of his looks and body, but even the attraction got old after a while, so he became more and more disgusting to her (and me). Jamie was the most conventional one, was obviously a good lover, and seemed to have the most staying power because he was serious. But he was angry at himself for loving Nola and not being able to have her on his own terms. Jamie wanted to win more than Mars and Greer did.

I think Spike Lee should be commended for the technical quality and aspects of this film, which contributed to how well he managed to tell his story. A lot of people don't realize just how many decisions have to be made before a film ever gets to the screen, and most of those decisions determine just how well you digest what you're being shown.

Motion is supposed to be the art of film, but it didn't take me long to adjust to Spike's presentation of still photographs. I thought the presentation was not only innovative but ingenious with respect to setting the tone and mood.

As is true in good fiction, the emotional impact of any film is derived from its truth, rather than just its beauty. *She's Gotta* wasn't what I'd call a pretty film, but the dramatic, comedic, and physical engagement with the human body made it beautiful to watch, so much so that I became unaware of the black and white within a few minutes of watching.

Fernando Solanas and Octavio Gettino, Third World filmmakers, have pointed out, "Every image that documents, bears witness to, refutes or deepens the truth of a situation is something more than a film image or purely artistic fact; it becomes something which the System finds indigestible."[1] Here I understand the term *system* to refer to white folks, especially those in Hollywood. This system is why it was so difficult for Spike Lee to get the backing to not only make this film but get it distributed. Distribution is crucial to a film. If no one knows about it, how can it possibly be seen? After *She's Gotta* was released, it opened in only three U.S. cities in a limited number of theaters, even though it had already garnered much attention at Cannes and elsewhere.

She's Gotta was a realistic film, and Spike Lee managed to reproduce the surface of reality with a minimum of distortion. He suggested the copiousness of life itself. Realism in film is a particular style, with physical reality as the source of all the raw materials of the film. If this film had been more in the formalist tradition and if Spike had deliberately stylized and distorted the truth and manipulated his images, I wouldn't have enjoyed this film so much. But here I think he has combined two forms.

It's been said that realist filmmakers try to capture the spontaneity of events and capture the flux of everyday occurrences. That they also aim for a rough look in their

[1] Quoted in Louis Giannetti, *Understanding Movies,* fifth edition (Englewood Cliffs, NJ: 1990).

images, one that doesn't prettify the materials with a self-conscious beauty of form. If it's too pretty, it's false. The subject matter is always supreme, and anything that distracts from the content is viewed by the filmmaker as superfluous. In its extreme form, the filmmaker ends up with a documentary or avant-garde cinema, which emphasizes technique, abstractions, and ideas, above and beyond concern for the characters' lives. I'm grateful that Spike Lee paid attention to the interior as well as exterior lives of his characters.

I have to tell you my most *favorite* scenes in the whole movie.

When Nola is in bed waiting for Greer to join her so that they can do the wild thing and Spike Lee lets the camera stay on Greer in real time as he takes his clothes off, neatly folding each item piece by piece—that just cracked me up.

The Thanksgiving dinner—I found it hard to believe but fun that all these guys would've actually stayed once they realized they'd all been invited.

But during that Scrabble game—when Greer got mad because Mars said "gonna" was a word but couldn't find it in the dictionary, and then Nola uses the word and Mars says, "See, I told you it was a word"—I died.

The dance scene was just perfect and sure enough depicted the push and pull that was going on between Jamie and Nola, although I still don't think Nola saw it that way.

When Mars calls Nola and she's in bed with old dead-ass Jamie, and Mars says, "Nola, just let me smell it!" I had tears in my eyes from laughing so hard.

But my most favorite scene of all was when Mars finally got a shot at it. Spike Lee put the lens on Nola's breasts, and we see how beautifully and tenderly Mars kisses and (well, you know) them. Spike Lee should cut this part of the film and send it to all the men who don't know what to do with a woman's breasts, because the noise made in that theater when we saw this happening was not just envy. We were grateful that her body was shown in such a beautiful, sensuous manner and appreciated by a black man who knew what to do with it.

I still have a few unanswered questions. For starters, why didn't they ever go out? All Nola ever did with these guys was do the wild thing. Greer was the only one who begged and pleaded with Nola to go somewhere, but the price was always so high (she'd have to be on her best behavior, dress a certain way, etc.). Other than that, not once do I remember them going to a concert or a movie. The bottom line is, it bees that way sometime. Most of their dates were under the covers and behind closed doors and they were free. What was it these men really saw in Nola? Was her stuff really that good? Did they realize that they were making fools of themselves? Did they know they were acting foolish?

I can't lie: at times, I wondered whether Nola Darling was a nympho. What did she actually want? Does she end up getting it? Who loses in this film, and who wins? And does it even matter? In the end Nola says, "I'm not a one-man woman" (though I don't believe her). The bottom line is, she's going to keep doing things her way until she does, by chance, stumble upon Mr. Right.

So, after all this, the bottom line is, I liked it. A lot.

The first read through. Spike had recently graduated
from New York University, but the school still allowed
him to use its facilities.

Facing page: (left to right) Bill Lee, Raye Dowell,
Epatha S. Merkinson, John Canada Terrell, Joie Lee,
Tracy Camila Johns, Tommy Redmond Hicks,
and Spike Lee.

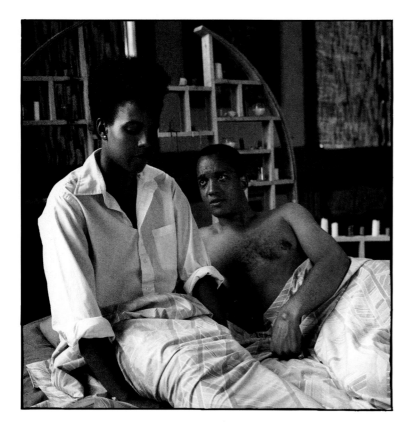

"Nola Darling," Tracy Camila Johns, and "Jamie Overstreet,"
Tommy Redmond Hicks.

Facing page: Nola's loft was on top of a restaurant, The Ferry Bank. The windows didn't open and it was 100 degrees without the lights on. Wynn Thomas, the production designer, got Nola's loving bed built. "At the time I remember being mad having to pay the extra hundred bucks for it," Spike recalls. "I told Wynn, I don't get it, any bed will do. I was dead wrong—with a capital W."

Spike and cameraman Ernest Dickerson.

"Opal Gilstrap," Raye Dowell.

Facing page: "Clorinda Bradford," Joie Lee.

Pages 36 and 37: Jamie calls Nola late at night, knowing
she's in her loving bed with somebody else.

The name "Mars" was suggested by Spike's
grandmother. She had a great uncle, Mars,
who was crazy.

Greer, Nola, Mars, and Jamie play Scrabble.

This scene in the film was composed of stills.

Nola and Jamie on a bench in Fort Greene Park.

She's Gotta Have It was the first of four films Joie Lee
(left) did with her brother. Tracy Camila Johns saw
Spike's ad for the role of Nola in *Back Stage*, sent in a
headshot, auditioned, and got the part.

Three men and a fine sister.

Bill Lee and bass. *She's Gotta Have It* was the third film
Spike's father had scored for him, after the student films
Sarah and *Joe's Bed-Stuy Barbershop: We Cut Heads.*

Facing page: Monty Ross and Spike met in 1975. They
both entered Morehouse College that August, but the
next year Monty transferred next door to Clark College.
"We used to sit on my grandmother's porch on those
hot, muggy Atlanta nights and talk about making
movies—what we are actually doing now."

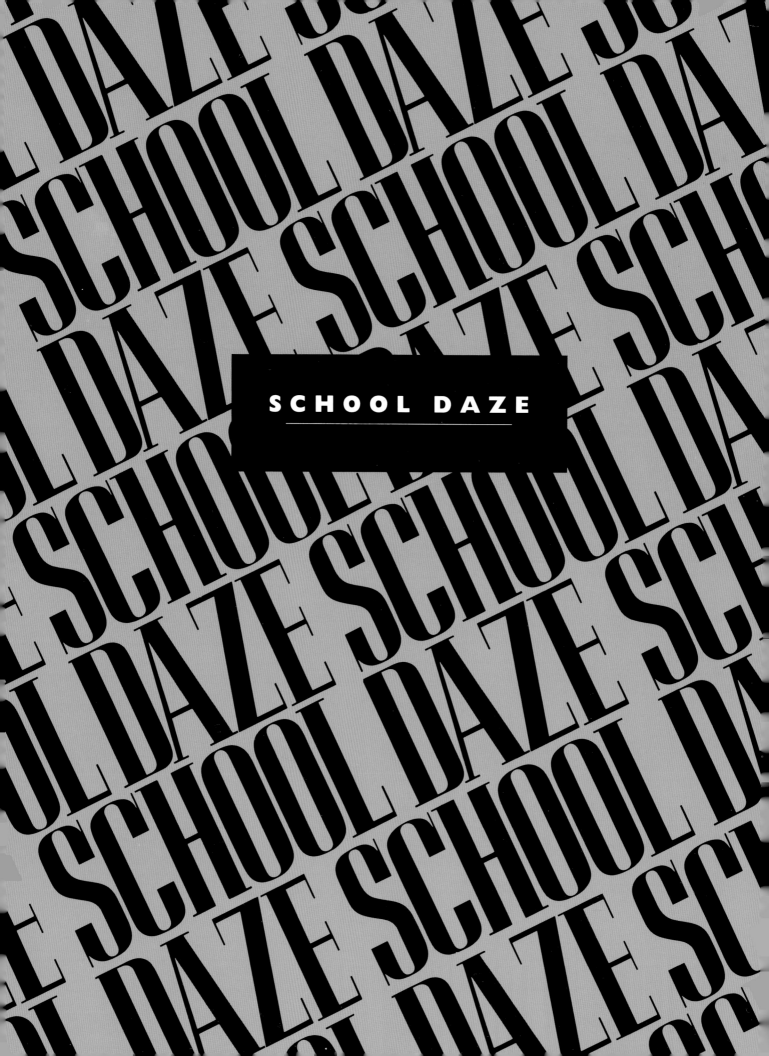

SCHOOL DAZE

PROGRAMMING WITH SCHOOL DAZE

TONI CADE BAMBARA

WE heard four things about *School Daze* during the spring of 1987 when Forty Acres and a Mule Filmworks was still on location in Atlanta: that it was a musical, that it was tackling the subject of color caste in the Black community, that it had an anti-apartheid theme, and that it was in trouble. The description was interesting; the bad news, of serious concern. In cases of studio-backed independent projects in trouble, Hollywood executives usually make the panicky decision to cut the elements that originally made the work compelling. Examples of films gutted of social relevance, formal innovations, or both are legion. That *School Daze* is not one of them is fortunate. Alert to the film's potential for countering the positive-images school's assertions that color bias played out decades ago and that "dirty laundry" is best kept in a lidded hamper anyway, community workers who use film in our practice were relieved by the late summer communiqué that *School Daze* was out of the woods. Programmers of independent film and video began planning how to use the new film to facilitate analyses of intra-community dynamics.

One of the many valuable things shared in the multiple-voiced casebook *Uplift the Race: The Construction of School Daze* (New York: Simon & Schuster, 1988) by Spike Lee and Lisa Jones is how to hang tough when beset by problems—the loss of critical location sites, the persistence of badmouthing rumors, severe plunges in morale, and competition with a production paying better rates for student extras. A Columbia Pictures executive dropped in for a mere minute then went home satisfied. And the production team brought the film in for a February 12, 1988, release. To the screen came a good-looking, ambitiously mounted, imaginatively designed production characterized by a bold mix of both dance and musical idioms and performatory and acting styles.

Set at a southern Black college during homecoming weekend, *School Daze* takes a serio-comic look at caste, class, and gender contradictions among four rival groups of students: Da Naturals, the Gamma Rays, Da Fellas, and the frat members and pledgees of Gamma Phi Gamma. "*West Side Story* with an apartheid twist," quipped a student DJ on WCLK radio in Atlanta. Whether the remark was facetiously or reverentially intended, *School Daze* is a house-divided pageant. It is a pageant in the sense that the spectacle inherent in traditional ceremonies and rites of homecoming (parades, floats, coronation balls, inductions into secret orders) provides the rationale for the overall style of the film.

It is a pageant, too, in the sense that confrontations between the groups are theatrically staged moments rather than realistic debates about the issues. The disturbances are broken up, either by an intervening character or by a scene shift, leaving the parties unreconciled and the contradictions unresolved. The function of the four groups of students is to enact the divisive behaviors that impede unification of the Black community. The film's agenda is to make a series of wake-up calls that the punnish title suggests is necessary for African folk asleep in the West.

The film begins as the Columbia Pictures logo is still on screen. On the sound track is the Middle Passage: the wheeze and creak of the ship plowing through water, the dip of the oars, the sounding of the ship's bell. As the prologue's first visual appears, the familiar black-and-white graphic of the slave ship, the old spiritual "I'm Building Me a Home" begins. Using archival materials, Lee presents a chronicle of a diasporized people's effort to make a home in the "new world." Several things are accomplished during the historical unfolding. A faux history is created for Mission College, the fictitious setting that functions as a micro-cosm. The viewer is reminded that much of our struggle in this land has been about the rights to literacy and autonomy and further that the educational institutions we have built are repositories for much of that history. The film also claims a position for itself in that history. Mission College becomes one of the "homes" alluded to in the spiritual "I'm Building Me a Home." The emancipatory enterprise, the Black nationalist quest for a collective "home," is presented from the time of Frederick Douglass to the era of the Black Panther Party. The prologue then segues to an anti-apartheid rally, the movie's opening scene, in which a Free Mandela banner waves. As *School Daze* unfolds, its depiction of contemporary tribal rites is informed by the Fanonian observation that when we internalize the enemy doctrine of supremacy, we jeopardize the liberation project.

Colorist, elitist, sexist, and heterosexist behaviors are presented—sometimes with a degree of hyperbole to signal satiric intent—through the four groups that constitute a hierarchy. The Gamma Phi Gamma forces command the most prestige and the most space on campus; also, they receive the most attention in the production (wardrobe, props, variety of settings, musical themes, spacious framing). Their agenda is to defend tradition at Mission and to perpetuate the prestige of their fraternity.

Committed to some degree to transforming tradition are members of the anti-apartheid forces, Da Fellas. Their homes on campus are the shanty town construction, a dorm room, and a second-hand car. Members of this group open and close the film and are the subjects of the longest sequence in the film.

The prestige of the Gamma Rays is derived from two sources, their "preferred" looks (light complexions, weave jobs, tinted contact lenses) and their position as the sister order of G Phi G. Their agenda is the maintenance of the frat: the Rays clean the frat house, assist the pledgees in their initiation tasks, throw parties for the brothers, and make themselves available for sex. Although their labor is indispensable to the maintenance of the frat, they are not; they are replaceable by other female recruits. For the most part, the Rays speak an odd form of ventriloquy and are treated by the film as well as by the frat as groupies.

Called Da Naturals in the casebook, Jigaboos on screen, and "Rachel and them" in spectator parlance is the group we come to know the least. Unorganized and with no discernible agenda, these brown-skinned, working-class sisters frequently utter non sequiturs and a variation of the ventriloquy scripted for the Rays. Their "home" is the dorm. Their members loll on a bed saying, "All men are dogs"; they shout from dorm windows saying, "All men are dogs."

In the intervals between group confrontations are several sketchy stories that function as the narrative outline: the seduction and corruption of a fugitive Jigaboo, Half-Pint (Spike Lee); the punishment of an ambitious Wannabee, Jane (Tisha Campbell); and the blown opportunity of a campus organizer, Dap (Larry Fishburne), to develop political coherence. The stories make useful points about intracommunity contradictions. Unfortunately, the film's agenda to make a wake-up call is undermined by the film's misogynistic and gay-hating sensibility.

Independent filmmaker Marlon Rigg responds to the homophobic bigotry in *School Daze* in his 1989 film *Tongues Untied*. A scripted performance-arts work about tribal rights and the tribal rights of Black gay men, *Untied* uses a clip from *Daze* in a section of the film that catalogues examples of heterosexist aggression by Black film and video makers. The clip is from the Greek show. Da Fellas launch into a call-and-response: "When I say Gamma, you say fag. Gamma (fag), Gamma (fag), Gamma, Gamma, Gamma, Gamma . . ." Da Fellas continue their disruption of the step contest by issuing threats to the fraternities they've labeled "fags"—"Get back or we'll kick your ass."

Lee's *School Daze*, Rigg's *Tongues Untied*, and Isaac Julien's *Looking for Langston* (a film frequently programmed with *Untied*)—each makes a claim on history while taking a position on the "dirty laundry" issue. *Daze* positions its statements on colorphobia and divisiveness as a counterpoise to the history of struggle chronicled in the prologue. *Untied*, through an innovative mix of idioms (autobiography, lyrical poetry, dramatic monologue, cinema-vérité-like scenarios, archival footage), challenges the attempt by the Black community to exclude its gay sector from Black radical history. Footage of gay rights marches is superimposed on footage of civil rights marches during the culmination of Rigg's assertive argument.

Looking is a meditation on Langston Hughes that uses the Harlem Renaissance as a cultural reference point for Black gay artists in Britain. Julien sets up a wished-for call-and-response between Harlem of the 1920s and southeast London of the 1980s. He uses archival materials, clothing, literary utterances, and period music to script the yearned-for dialogue. The quest by contemporary Black gay poets for an ancestor, a forefather, a tradition, a past has to override a double silence: Langston Hughes disclosed little about his sexual identity, and the executors of the Hughes estate demanded, in addition to various cuts, that Hughes's voice be lowered on the sound track.

Tradition, Mission College's and the G Phi G fraternity's, is what Julian/Big Brother Almighty (Giancarlo Esposito) continually uses as his source of authority, especially in his war with Da Fellas. The radical tradition that Dap could invoke to strengthen his position is not honored at Mission. The three films together—*Daze, Untied,* and *Looking*—make for an excellent program on the issue of negotiating identity, individual and collective, in spite of invisibilized histories.

School Daze is a musical. It does not operate like an old MGM down-on-your-heels/up-on-your-toes sis-boom-bah on a mock set of Claremont College. It is not "good news" on campus that *Daze* is singing and dancing about. More is at stake at Mission than whether Grady (Bill Nunn) makes a touchdown. The college is being held hostage by the "old money" robber barons. A wake-up call occurs in a scene in which the chairperson of the board of trustees (Art Evans) advises the president of the college (Joe Seneca) to squash the student-led divest-now campaign because the venerable personages who finance the college will not tolerate being told where they may or may not invest their money. Actor Evans laments, "Why won't our people support our institutions?" At the time of *Daze*'s filming, Cheney and Fisk were being bailed out of serious financial difficulty.

Lee, to make a wake-up call about intracommunity self-ambush, chooses an enshrined genre of the dominant cinema, musical comedy, whose conventions were not designed to address an embattled community's concerns. Much of the tension on screen derives from his effort to link two opposing discourses: will the ideological imperatives of Lee's agenda subvert the genre, or will the ideological imperatives of the genre derail his agenda? The linchpin is the cinematic rhetoric (framing, choreographed moves, delivery of choral ensemble, costuming) surrounding the fraternity that links the generic conventions (say, spectacle) to the critique of community divisiveness. The story is grounded in Afro-centric modes and idioms (homecoming events, Da Butt, all-up-in-your-face-isms), as are the devices Lee habitually draws from French bedroom farce, nouvelle vague, and Scorsese, as well as from independents who work outside of the industry. "Face," which has become a Lee signature, for example, is the visual equivalent of the oral tradition that resonates in the opening phrase of Toni Morrison's novel *The Bluest Eye:* "Quiet as it's kept . . ."

The rival groups at the college are repeatedly in each other's face. In the scene at the women's dorm when Half-Pint attempts to get a date, Lee goes beyond using main-stream film devices—talk, shot-response, shot—so that a series of women appear who say, without having to actually articulate it, "Get out of my face." When Dap figuratively gets in Da Fellas' face because Da Fellas prefer to go to the dance rather than keep a vigil in the shanty town, they in turn get in our face: "Lighten up, Marcus Garvey," "Preach, Jesse," "Chill, Farrakhan," "Teach, Malcolm." The close-ups in this scene reconnect us to the history in the prologue, reminding us of what is at stake. The "face" device is responsible, in part, for the intimacy Lee establishes between filmmaker, film, and spectator.

Lee's decision to link old conventions with new ones allows him to deliver pleasure in some of the forms by which dominant cinema keeps audiences addicted to voyeurism, fetishism, spectacle, mystifying notions of social relations, and freakish notions of intimate relations. The mix also allows Lee to present characters in their milieu and to address socially relevant issues, both of which the dominant cinema rules out. What is lost in the mix is the opportunity to articulate a radical Black discourse. What is gained is the opportunity to position several types of spectators.

Since the test case of television's *All in the Family,* commercial success has depended on the ability of an entertainment industry product to address a polarized audience. White reactionaries seeing themselves on prime time were affirmed in their bigotry. White liberals, reading the show as an exposé, congratulated the inventors of Archie Bunker on their "prog-ress." Many Black people, desperately needing to see any sign of US Bunkerism defanged, tuned in each week to crack and to reassure each other.

Sexist/gynophobes, heterosexist/homophobes, and other witting and unwitting defenders of patriarchy champion Spike Lee films. So do nonreactionaries. So do many pro-gressives. Not because the texts are so malleable that they can be maneuvered into any given ideological space, but because many extratextual elements figure into the response. Hunger for images is one element; pride in Lee's accomplishment is another. That the range of spectators is wide speaks to the power of the films and the brilliance of the filmmaker.

Many spectators are willing to provide the interrogation missing in the representa-tions on screen because of progressive features: ensemble (collective) playing, the mutually supportive affection of Dap and Rachel (Kyme), the themes of color and apartheid, the pro-Afro esthetic of Da Butt, and the cast mix of veterans, newcomers, and performers known in other media. Many spectators do not view the film as separate from the figure, Spike Lee, behind it, or the emerging movement that figure is a part of.

The message of *Daze* for large numbers of spectators is entrepreneurial, cultural, political, and emblematic of the resurgence of African-American expression by the genera-tion that came of age in the post-1960s era. The mixed-strategy approach in the Lee films has released a voice the dominant industry would prefer silenced—the B-boys. Lee's composite push (T-shirts, books, and sound-track CDs) has helped to create a breakthrough for various forms of cultural expression in the marketplace. His commercial success has helped to create a climate of receptivity for Black filmmakers in Hollywood. His preparation of audiences for more active spectatorship is a boon to hundreds of independent Black filmmakers and videographers working in the independent sector.

The color issue is introduced early in *Daze* in a robust production number called "Good and Bad Hair" ("Straight and Nappy" in the casebook). The two groups of sisters encounter each other in the dormitory hallway; neither will give way. Jane, a blonde with green contact lenses, accuses Rachel, a brown-skinned sister with a short 'fro, of having eyes for her boyfriend, Julian. The others, meanwhile, are cracking on one another's weave jobs, kinks, and attitudes. The close-up is held on the two actresses, Kyme and Campbell, in each other's face. Their cohorts call one another Jigaboos and Wannabees. The face-off triggers a production number in a beauty parlor called Madame Ree Ree's. There the women sing and dance a *femme de guerre* to a 1940s-style big-band swing composition with fall-out lyrics.

The Rays and Da Naturals encounter each other several times. The behavior never varies; they sling color-hair insults, but nothing develops. With the exception of a pained remark Rachel makes to Dap after she has a run-in with Jane, no attempt is made in the film to explore, say, the cost of this pro-racist pathology. Such an exploration could have occurred in three scenes involving Rachel and her roommates (Alva Rogers and Joie Lee), but instead they discuss "men are dogs." And it could have also occurred in one scene involving Jane and the other Rays, but instead they plan a party for the frat brothers.

Colorism is reintroduced as a subject in scenes between Rachel and Dap. Dap does not support Rachel's plan to pledge Delta. "They do good work in the community," she argues. Dap, a campus organizer, is opposed. Sororities are as bad as fraternities, he maintains, although he's helped his cousin Half-Pint pledge. Dap's denunciations include charges of color prejudice. She accuses Dap of being equally color struck, belligerent as he is about light-skinned folks. She teases him too about his claims of being pure African. When he won't relent, it occurs to her that his attraction to her may be PR motivated. "Having one of the darker sisters on campus as your girlfriend is good for your all the way Black nationalist image," she says and exits. Although Dap and Rachel get together again, no further mention is made of her charge.

Not verbally stated but visually presented, color caste combined with gender and class operate in the story of Daryl/Half-Pint. He has working-class origins and middle-class ambitions. The viewer's attention is frequently called to the fact that he is brown-skinned, short, and spare by his placement among light-skinned and husky fellow pledgees and among light-skinned and "healthy" sisters. To "graduate" from a less-privileged caste to a more-privileged caste as a member of the reigning fraternity, Half-Pint perseveres in a grueling regimen. The pledgees wear dog collars and chains; they get down on all fours and bark like dogs; they gobble Alpo on command from pet bowls; they drop their pants to be whacked with a mammoth paddle. Half-Pint is singled out by the president of the campus chapter, Julian/Big Brother Almighty, for taunts about his "manhood." To enter G Phi G, the pledgees will be branded. We see Julian's huge, ugly scar of a "G" during one of his scenes with Jane.

The seduction and corruption of Half-Pint culminate in his participation in sexual treachery engineered by Julian. It is gender coercion—"You're a pussy," "Only a Gamma man is a real man and a real man ain't no virgin"—that drives Half-Pint into the men-as-predators/women-as-prey brotherhood. His supremacist-warped agenda to flee his social origins led him to G Phi G. The extravagant attention that the movie gives the frat forces in terms of production and design makes the seduction and corruption of Half-Pint plausible.

The depiction of the fraternity's abusive order and of Half-Pint's ordeal makes a good argument for men engaging in the feminist enterprise of dismantling patriarchy. But what is made more visible in the film is the vested interest men (and women) have in an order characterized by male power, prestige, and prerogative.

The topic predictably raised in postscreening discussions by spectators who identify with Half-Pint is society's standard of male attractiveness. Art Nomura in his video "Wok Like a Man" tackles the implications of the Euro-American standard of height, weight, and aggression for Asian men. On screen and off, one way to become attractive is to have social power or prestige through male bonding, most usually in terms of a shared sexist socialization to despise and exploit women.

Alien standards of beauty internalized at great psychic cost by African-Americans are taken up in Ayoka Chenzira's provocative short *Hairpiece: A Film for Nappy-Headed People*. The politics of color links such works as Julie Dash's *Illusions*, Denise Oliver and Warrington Hudlin's *Color*, Henry Miller's *Death of a Dunbar Girl*, Maureen Blackwood's *A Perfect Image?*, Shu Lea Cheang's *Color Schemes*, and Ana Maria Garcia's *Cocolos y Roqueras*. The politics of female representation is treated in Sharon Alile Larkin's *A Different Drummer*. And the complexity and subjectivity of women's experiences is the forte of Zeinbai Davis, Camille Billops, Michelle Parkerson, and Barbara McCullough. These issues are central to discussions about the presentation of Jane (Tisha Campbell). The bases of her characterization are classic features in the construction of the feminine: narcissism, masochism, and hysteria. Her seductive display at the ball singing "I Don't Want to Be Alone Tonight," her ambition, and her voluntary sacrifice ("I did what you told me, Julian") are classic she-was-asking-for-it features of femocidal texts.

Uplift the Race informs us that in the original script the frat members entered the Boning Room and ran a train on Jane. Apparently, the thinking behind this particular wake-up call went like this: isn't it a drag the way men get over on women and how women allow themselves to be ripped off, so let's sock it to this character Jane to protest the unfair situation. Yeah right. But the appearance of intended meaning (protest) fails to mask the constructed meaning (punishment).

When the Lee films are programmed together, a disturbing pattern emerges. Posters of naked women nailed to the wall in Joe's place of business in *Joe's Bedstuy Barber Shop: We Cut Heads* reappear in *Mo' Better Blues* as pictures the musicians pass around while telling one of the guys he should dump his white lover and get himself "an African queen." They hand him pictures of naked Black women. In *Daze*, a male character says "pussy" in one scene, and in the next the Gamma Rays say "Meow." A more frightening continuity exists between the gratuitous attack of the woman on the stairs in *Joe's*; the rough-off of Nola in *She's Gotta Have It*, an act assuaged by her term "near rape"; and the scapegoating of Jane in *Daze* after she appears in a porno-referenced sex scene with Julian.

Jane is drawn in the conventional pattern of sexual iconography that hallmarks the industry. Gender issues receive no better treatment in *Daze* than in usual commercial fare.

But the possibility, and perhaps the intent, were present. The repetitive and exaggerated attention that Lee gives to statements like "a real man," for example, beginning with the first entrance of the frat and the pledgees, sets us up for an exploration that is merely sketched by the comparison-contrast between Julian and Dap—their styles of leadership and how they maintain intimate relationships. What a "real woman" might be is never raised, and little attention is given to the characterizations of female characters.

It was not necessary, of course, to have the frat brothers run a train on Jane. Their presence outside the door and their readiness to go in and "check out how Half-Pint's doing" are suggestive enough of gang rape, particularly after the earlier command was given to Half-Pint to bring "a freak" back to the dorm. It will take another kind of filmmaker, perhaps, to move to the next step and illuminate the homoeroticism-homophobia nexus at play in gang rape and in the kind of surveillance engaged in by the frat brothers, and in the kind of obsessing Mars, Jamie, and Childs engage in about each other through Nola in *Gotta*. Dap's character doesn't articulate the simple wisdom that gay-hate and dominance aren't really crucial to male development. Dap jams his cousin, but he welcomes Julian into the inner circle of the final wake-up call in the film. Would that there had been as much attention paid to human values as to production values.

The anti-apartheid theme is introduced in *Daze*'s opening scene. It is the first wake-up call. "We're late," Dap informs the student body assembled around the administration building. Other universities have been pressured to divest, but Mission hasn't. Dap urges the students to take action: to march, to disrupt classes, to stage a sit-down, and, if necessary, to close the school down. He is drowned out by offscreen chanting—"It takes a real man to be a Gamma man and only a Gamma man is a real man." The frat marches the pledgees onto the turf; they disrupt the rally, seize the space, and disperse the crowd. Within seconds Dap and Julian are in each other's face; in the background, visible between the close-up of the two actors, is a Free Mandela banner. Virgil (Gregg Burge), the student council president, steps in between Dap and Julian and breaks them up. A similar scene occurs during the homecoming parade when Julian takes exception to the introduction of a political banner by Da Fellas at traditional festivities. Virgil steps in again and breaks them up. In pay back, Dap and Da Fellas disrupt the Greek Show and bogart the step contest. We assume that their performance will reintroduce the anti-apartheid theme. It does not. Instead it reasserts an aggressive machismo ("Daddy Lonnnngstroke . . ." "Get back or we'll kick your Gamma ass . . ." "When I say Alpha, you say punk").

A link, though, is made between South African apartheid and the US sharecropping system. It occurs at the top of the longest, most emotionally varied sequence in the film. This sequence is an audience favorite. Dap insists the Da Fellas help him defy the ban issued by the administration. Booker T. (Eric A. Payne) 'lows as how he's not risking being expelled by continuing in the divest-now campaign. He's the first in his family ever to go to college; his family "slaved" to get him there. Dap tries to get him to see that the situations are related, that apartheid is international. Da Fellas walk, fed up with Dap, who speaks of the campaign as a personal mission and of their participation as proof of their loyalty and friendship to him (shades of Julian's "Do you love me, Jane? Well, you're going to have to prove it"). He murdermouths them as they exit. Sulking, he hurls a dart at the board. There's a knock on the door. Dap opens it. Piled in cartoon fashion against the doorjamb are Da Fellas. "Do revolutionaries eat Kentucky Fried Chicken?" Grady wants to know.

At Kentucky Fried Chicken, Jordan (Branford Marsalis) leaves the table in search of the salt. A shaker is on a table occupied by local working-class brothers. A local in a cap (Samuel Jackson) is relating some off-the-wall anecdote about how he had to get some "bitch" straight. (A few sisters in the audience suck our teeth. We've been assaulted thus far by "freak," "pussy," "tits and bootays," "meow," "bitch"—and the night is still relatively young.) Jordan asks for the salt. The locals look him up and down and continue to talk. Dap calls Jordan back to the table. The local in the cap calls over in falsetto, "Is it true what they say about Mission [limp wrist] 'men'?" This is the umpteenth anti-gay remark. Dap suggests they leave; Da Fellas grumble but get up. (Members of the audience holler because Da Fellas are leaving behind all that chicken!)

In the parking lot, Dap leads Da Fellas to the car. Edge (Kadeem Hardison) does not want to retreat; he's ready to throw down. In seconds, the two groups are lined up in a face-off. The guy in the cap lets it be known that the locals are sick and tired of college boys coming on their turf every year and treating them like dirt. On-campus distinctions between Jigaboos and Wannabees are of no importance to the locals; all college types are Wannabees and ought to stay on campus where they belong. "On account of you college boys, we can't get jobs, and we were born here," the actor Jackson says, cutting through the artifice of the staging. The actors strain to stay on their marks, adding to the electrical charge of the scene. Stuck, Da Fellas go for the short hairs. Dap cracks on the "'Bama country ass" locals' shower caps and Jerri curls and casts aspersions on their manhood. Jordan chimes in with "bitch" here and "bitch" there. The local in red pleather (Al Cooper) endures it all with a stony gaze. His partner (Jackson) resumes his assault—"You're all niggers, just like us." He and Dap are face to face. No student council president is present to intervene. Dap steps in closer and says, "You're not niggers." There's a helpless quality to the delivery; there's a vulnerability to the moment. What is at stake for the entire community that refuses to wake up is sounded here. The scene shifts.

Da Fellas are quiet and reflective in the car. So are spectators in the movie seats. Monroe (James Bond III) breaks the silence: "Do we really act like that?" Dap swears it's a case of mistaken identity. Jordan launches into a "I'm Bennett and I ain't in it" routine. Grady has no sympathy for "losers." He is challenged on the class issue. Things are about to disrupt, but Monroe makes a cornball remark that gives them an out. Da Fellas, relieved, pound on Monroe while Booker T. maintains a grip on the steering wheel. Spotting Julian and Jane, Dap jumps out and jumps right in Julian's chest, saying Julian better make sure that Half-Pint gets into the frat. We've now seen Dap blow the opportunity to develop political clarity three times: with Rachel, when she challenges him on the color question; with Da Fellas, when they suggest that one of the reasons they won't back him is his personality; with the locals, when they let it be known that the debate between the Greeks and campus revolutionaries has no explanatory power in the lives of most Black folks.

The film's finale begins moments after Half-Pint beats on Dap and Grady's door to announce that he is now a "real man." The next scene takes place in hazy yellow light. Images are stretched. Movement is slowed down. In a wide-angle close-up, Dap shouts "Waaake Uuuupp." Fishburne here displays his vocal register in the exact way that Esposito has done in previous scenes. Does this signal concord between the two male groups? The college bell is ringing. The entire school rises and goes to the quad. Julian gets out of bed where he's been sleeping with one of Jane's sorors (Jasmine Guy). He is the last to arrive. The camera adopts Julian's point of view as he moves through the crowd toward Dap. Actor Esposito has a particular expression; it may imply that the character has become aware of his ability to change. As the camera ascends, Dap and Julian turn to us and Dap says, "Please, wake up."

Within weeks of its release, *Daze* became the subject of extravagant claims by folks who'd seen it and loved it, who'd seen it and not liked it, and who hadn't checked it out yet but had their ear cocked to Communitysay: *School Daze* is going to do more to increase enrollment at Black colleges than an army of recruiters could; *School Daze* is going to outshine "The Mind Is a Terrible Thing to Waste" campaigns for gift giving to Black institutions; *School Daze* is going to revitalize our fraternities, and brothers are going to be stepping all over Harvard Yard. By summer—without recourse to stats or surveys and frequently without recourse to a screening of the film—Peoplesay dropped its prophesizing tone, and the statements rang with conviction.

Conversations in neighborhood movie houses focused briefly on the apartheid theme and the range of contradictions treated in *Daze*. Most of the excitement had to do with Lee's original impulse to make use of his experiences as a Morehouse College undergraduate. Aysha Simmons, former Swarthmore student, recalls that despite passionate dissatisfaction with the film's sexism and heterosexism, the overwhelming feeling within her circle was envy: "We envied the social life of a Black campus." Elvin Rogers, formerly of the University of Pennsylvania, echoes Simmons: "The hazing practices were horrifying, but after seeing the movie we wanted to enroll in a Black college."

Communitysay's claims weren't farfetched. Many Black colleges and organizations actually did raise funds in a direct way with screenings of *Daze*. And Black Greeks did commence to step all over the quads at Princeton, Harvard, and Yale. And although the various federal agencies and foundations that commission studies of Black colleges and universities can't support a causality theory, preliminary reports from the United States Office of Education, the United States National Center for Education Statistics, and the Carnegie Foundation do show an unprecedented spurt in Black college enrollment, in Black student enrollment, and in gift giving in the past two-year period. And according to television newscasts during the Thanksgiving holiday of 1990, the Atlanta University complex has been overwhelmed by applications from transfer students and first-year enrollees. In all probability, the 1990 report from the Research Department of the United Negro College Fund will tell the tale more precisely.

The rest of the story is for the audience to report. The Lee films insist on an active spectatorship by the kinds of questions they pose. *School Daze* asks, so what are we going to do about this color/class thaang? Or as the student council president demanded to know at the homecoming parade confrontation, "What do you want to do—kill each other?"

Special thanks to a number of friends for good talks: Louis Massiah; Cheryl Chisholm; Mantia Diawara; Clyde Taylor; the screeners of the Scribe Video Center in Philly and the African American Culture Institute of the University of Pennsylvania, and the Black Student Association at the University of California at Santa Cruz (Oakes College); students at Howard University, Spelman College, Knoxville College, the University of Ohio in Columbus; Mrs. Beatty's senior English class at East Austin High in Knoxville, Tennessee; the sisters with the cassette player at the laundromat on Chelten Avenue and Pilasky Street in Philly; and the brothers with the VCR at the Metropolitan Pool Hall near the Intervale Avenue El in the Bronx.

Phyllis Stickney and Vanessa Williams were originally cast as "Rachel Meadows" and "Jane Toussaint." Because of artistic differences, they were replaced.

The two who got the parts—Kyme and Tisha Campbell.

Jesse Jackson says a prayer for the success of *School Daze* at the commencement of production. Spike and Jesse stand with *School Daze* coproducer Monty Ross (left) and executive producer Grace Blake (right).

Da Fellas.

Gammites.

Jigaboos.

Wannabees.

Choreographer Otis Sallid shows how to do that
coon dance.

The Wannabees do "Hattie McDaniels."

Facing page: Jane Toussaint and Rachel Meadows fight it
out via dance in the "Straight and Nappy" number.

Gamma Phi Gamma.

Facing page: Static between Da Fellas and Local Yokels.

"Lizzie Life," Joie Lee, and "Doris Witherspoon,"
Alva Rogers.

Facing page: "Coach Odom," Ossie Davis, fires up
his football team.

Shooting the ballet number.
(It was eventually cut from the film.)

Facing page: The Gamma Rays sing "Be Alone Tonight."

Pages 70 and 71: Doing "Da Butt."

"Wake Up."

Setting up the "Wake Up" finale.

"WAKE UP!"

Ernest Dickerson rides the CINE-JIB crane.

The Crew. Being a Morehouse man going back to film at his alma mater, Spike thought he would be welcomed with open arms. That wasn't the case. Morehouse kicked the production team off campus. They finished at Atlanta University.

DO THE RIGHT THING: FILM AND FURY

NELSON GEORGE

> Between 1950 and 1957 alone, Brooklyn lost a total of 135,000 men, women, and children. They were buying the blarney about the suburbs, they were buying cars, they were moving out to the sticks. Filling the housing vacuum they left behind 100,000 newcomers moved in, many of them black and Puerto Rican, many also seeking a better tomorrow, as their predecessors had. Another wave of resettlement for Brooklyn. —Elliot Willensky, *When Brooklyn Was the World: 1920–1957*

THE CITY

YOU can't fully appreciate *Do the Right Thing* (1989) until you learn a thing or two about Brooklyn. In the good old days, before an overpriced high rise replaced Ebbets Field, Brooklyn's tribalism was a cute national joke. All those Jews, Italians, and Irish in Flatbush, Bushwick, Red Hook, and beyond rubbed up against one another and spoke an endearing local patois that inspired hundreds of whimsical anecdotes, a bunch of musicals, and the creation of television's favorite proletarians—bus driver Ralph Kramden and his sewer-working pal Ed Norton. Even today, some of New York's best-known columnists—Pete and Denis Hamill, Mike McAlary, Jimmy Breslin—write (and think) with a Brooklyn accent; a nostalgia for the Dodger days runs deep among news editors; and in Bay Ridge, New Utrecht, and Bensonhurst, the people who remember the old Brooklyn get dewy-eyed over names like O'Dwyer and Furillo and Steingut.

In today's Brooklyn, the Irish, Italians, and Jews are players but no longer the whole game. They are now forced to share Brooklyn with Jamaicans, Dominicans, Puerto Ricans, African-Americans, Haitians, Iranians, and Koreans. And every year since the Dodgers bolted, these black, brown, and yellow peoples have swelled and shifted, moving from Bedford-Stuyvesant down through Crown Heights, East Flatbush, and Flatbush, and west from East New York and Brownsville into Canarsie toward Mill Basin. The residents of the remaining white homelands have responded to this new social mix by running away or watching ruefully as their European enclaves turn into Third World villages. And although the white media still haven't realized it, the West Indian-American Day parade is New York's biggest ethnic celebration, not just in the borough, but in the city—and yes, it is larger than the St. Patrick's Day parade.

Racial antagonisms and a rising tide of black nationalism accompanied the change in population. The African-American community, led by black activists, responded vociferously not only to the notorious murders of two young black men in the white enclaves of Howard Beach and Bensonhurst but to every slight blacks suffered at the hands of whites. This rage and nationalism combined to inspire a desire for community control.

The background of settlement and resettlement in Brooklyn and consequent antagonisms sheds light on the events depicted in *Do the Right Thing*. By integrating the history and sociology of his hometown into this work, Spike Lee has made a film that works as idiosyncratic art and powerful social commentary.

THE FILM

In the hot summer of 1989, Sal's Famous Pizzeria is the last outpost of old ethnic colonialism in the heart of predominantly black Bedford-Stuyvesant. Just a few years earlier, most small businesses in Bed-Stuy were white owned. But things had changed. Aggressive new immigrants had moved in, creating a new cadre of merchants such as the Korean couple whose grocery store is just across the street from Sal's. Thus, the exchange for services rendered arises not only when black residents purchase pizzas from Sal or when he pays Mookie $250 for delivering pizzas, but when blacks buy beer or batteries from the Korean grocer. The three ethnic groups—black, Italian, and Korean—engage daily in a balancing act of self-interest, with the exchange of money for services camouflaging larger economic issues and social conflicts. Lee presents not only a political perspective but also his personal point of view, which enables a feisty Puerto Rican woman, a patronizing Italian pizza maker, and a melancholy African-American matron to have their say.

One of the film's most articulate voices is provided not by a character but by the music of Public Enemy—the explosive "Fight the Power." This music is also the spine of *Do the Right Thing*, with Public Enemy participating as an unseen Greek chorus that comments on the film's action. Using a James Brown beat and a dense mix of sampled and played instruments, the Bomb Squad (Hank and Keith Shocklee, Eric Sadler, and Carlton Reidenhour) created a music so intense it sounds like the black revolt many of the film's critics anticipated. Public Enemy's Chuck Dee and Flavor Flav convey the reason for the maelstrom—"Our freedom of speech is really freedom of death"—and set a tone of contempt—"Elvis was a racist, simple and plain / motherfuck him and John Wayne."

Despite several rap movies before *Do the Right Thing*, no previous film had effectively used hip hop's rhythm and intensity to enhance its drama. Depending on where it's placed in the film, the rap has varied meanings. In the opening credits, with the song pulsating as Tina (Rosie Perez) gyrates, it establishes a vibrant, rebelliously celebratory tone. Heard on the portable cassette player of Radio Raheem (Bill Nunn) as he moves through Bedford-Stuyvesant, it works a sonic wuf ticket the hulking Raheem can back up. To the folks on the block the song articulates Raheem's potency and potential for violence. To Sal (Danny Aiello) the rap is a manifestation of the wild and disrespectful behavior of blacks. It fires up Raheem and the militant Buggin' Out (Giancarlo Esposito) when they finally decide to confront Sal about the absence of African-Americans from his Wall of Fame. And in the fateful shouting match at the pizzeria, where Raheem's and Sal's desire for respect conflict, it's the wailing of "Fight the Power" that foreshadows the violence.

The violence escalates through a series of events: the Sal and Raheem battle, the street fight on the pizzeria's doorstep, the subduing and murder of Raheem by the police, the decision to leave the Koreans alone, and Mookie's decision to destroy Sal's. While watching those events, most viewers were stunned, not enraged. Unlike the designer gore of action flicks that encourages audiences to cheer body count, the violence in *Do the Right Thing* invites a feeling of uneasiness as characters the audience cares about make wrong, life-rupturing decisions. It is not cartoon mayhem. It can be characterized as spur-of-the-moment aggression, echoing what occurred in Bensonhurst and Howard Beach. It is the kind of reactionary violence that changes lives and divides cities.

One of the controversies surrounding the film is whose life is more valuable, Sal's or Raheem's? Many writers implied that Raheem's death didn't outweigh the destruction of Sal's store. These comments reveal more about the writers than about the film. That Sal had more lines, a business, and two kids didn't make him any more humane a character than Raheem. For most of the African-Americans who viewed *Do the Right Thing,* especially younger urban viewers, Raheem—a taciturn brother who used his size and box to ward off others—was a schoolmate, neighbor, cousin, brother, or even themselves. Although not loved by all the folks on the block, to them, and most black viewers, he's a person, not an animal. People with a mainstream (or middle-class or white) outlook view young African-Americans with ghetto blasters as public nuisances whose presence challenges society's standards. To anyone familiar with Public Enemy's logo of a black teen in a police gun sight, Raheem is the living embodiment of that image.

Lee developed his characters as both people and archetypes. Raheem, and his music, represent the brooding masses of misunderstood, often hostile youths of our big cities. Buggin' Out is Raheem's homeboy. He articulates his political grievances and is enraged by Sal's all-Italian Wall of Fame. Like any activist leader, he sees a problem (the Wall of Fame), attempts to organize masses (the block), is ignored by most, and then leads the converted (Raheem and Smiley) in an act of civil disobedience (the confrontation at Sal's).

Da Mayor (Ossie Davis) and Sister Mother (Ruby Dee) are longtime residents of the block, whose accents reveal their southern roots. Da Mayor, an alcoholic, is essentially a good man. His rescue of the child from the speeding car illustrates that. But he's so beaten down by personal failure that he has given up on life. Sister Mother watches everything, has opinions of everyone, but mostly keeps her own counsel. Like many older New Yorkers, she seems saddened by and distanced from the world that now surrounds her.

Smiley (Roger Smith), the seller of magic-marker embellished photos of Malcolm X with Martin Luther King, Jr., is the block's frustrated griot—a keeper of the historical flame who draws political pictures but whose speech impairment prevents him from conveying his message to others. Jade (Joie Lee) is the hard-working black woman who attempts to look beyond racism and will not tolerate it as an excuse for laziness. Sal represents every paternalistic member of an old-line New York ethnic group who has a kind but condescending view of his customers. That he feels they are childlike and irresponsible is apparent in his dealings with Da Mayor and Mookie (Spike Lee), and in his refusal to include African-Americans on his Wall of Fame.

Pino (John Turturro), Sal's hot-tempered son, is one of Lee's most delicious creations—an outspoken racist who is also a product of media integration. Although he views African-Americans as inferior, his pop-culture life is jammed with sepia superheroes like Magic Johnson, Prince, and Eddie Murphy. (One of the ironies of the post-civil rights era is that the wide acceptance of black stardom hasn't really changed ground-level racism—something King had hoped for, but Malcolm X had anticipated.) The Korean store owners are the new "others" whose presence in Bed-Stuy causes African-Americans to question their own initiative and prejudices.

Center stage in *Do the Right Thing* is Lee's most complex and important character, the pizza messenger, Mookie. As laconically portrayed by Lee, Mookie is a man stuck uneasily in the middle. "Yo, Mookie stay black!" Buggin' Out warns him after being removed from Sal's. Seconds later inside the shop Sal tells him, "I'm the boss!" The Jackie Robinson jersey that Mookie wears does not suggest that he's a racial pioneer but that he's a man watched closely by interested parties on both sides of the racial divide. Both sides think he's loyal to them—that's how he survives. Yet Mookie is in essence that self-centered, irresponsible, narrow-minded black man of innumerable sociological essays. Paid "Two fifty! Cash money!" a week, homey actually thinks he's cold gettin' paid. But even he must really know it's only off-the-books chump change. His dependence on his sister Jade for shelter and avoidance of his responsibilities as a father to little Hector and as Tina's man reveal his irresponsible life-style and portend his limited future.

Going against the traditions of Hollywood films and the wishes of many blacks seeking positive images, Lee endowed his central character with some foul personality traits and challenged the sympathies of his African-American fans. Because Mookie is not a traditional hero, his decision to throw the garbage can through Sal's window isn't an obvious cheer inducer. Although it's a reaction to Raheem's death, it's also a by-product of his own personal frustrations, including his underlying lack of self-esteem. "Hate!" Mookie is a victim of and catalyst for hate—racial, economic, and personal.

Like the perpetrators of New York's other celebrated acts of racial violence, Mookie has no rational explanation for his behavior, only that for a moment he was overcome by a feeling, a real bad feeling, that he acted on (as did the block's residents and the police and fire departments). This kind of violence can be characterized as a fever that overwhelms one's better judgment. And it is this hateful fever that Lee captures in as harrowing a series of scenes as is found in contemporary American cinema.

Heroes are hard to find in *Do the Right Thing* but easy to find offscreen. For example, the cinematographer, Ernest Dickerson, deserves much praise. The slightly off-kilter camera angles, the fluid movements up and down the block, and the vibrant colors of the film are all wonderful. In addition, the skin tones of the black cast are as rich and varied as they are in real life. Another hero is Wynn Thomas, who provided marvelously textured designs for the block—Sal's pizzeria, WE LOVE Radio, and the Korean grocery. Both Dickerson and Thomas were crucial in achieving the look that made *Do the Right Thing* so memorable.

Because Lee doesn't devote himself solely to plot, his films have an experimental, nonmainstream quality. An important element of *Do the Right Thing,* and all of Lee's films, are what might be called Spikeisms—devices sprinkled throughout the feature that stop the narrative yet reinforce the film's theme. For instance, Lee loves to have people talk to the camera—he's had such scenes in all his works. In the middle of *Do the Right Thing,* characters hurl bitter, funny racial slurs at the audience; these slurs suggest the real hatred that underlies racial and ethnic humor and underscore the tension building within the story. Another example is Lee's use of a minimusical essay in which Señor Love Daddy (Sam Jackson) provides a roll call of black musical greats in the middle of the film. Some critics termed the roll call gratuitous, but this is just another one of the touches that gives Lee's work its unique personality.

Do the Right Thing often feels whimsical because Lee's natural gift for humor is an essential tool in introducing and humanizing his characters. Casting the brilliant comic Robin Harris as one of the corner men guaranteed laughter. But all the jokes have edgy punch lines that illuminate either character or aspects of racial intolerance. For all his humorous instincts Lee isn't satisfied with making a straight commercial comedy. In Do the Right Thing he successfully incorporates his comic talents in a story so topical it became a factor in the 1989 New York mayoral election. When you consider its overall artistry and impact at the time of its release, this is the Spike Lee joint that will be studied well after the year 2000. And, as Señor Love Daddy would say, "That's the truth, Ruth!"

The sign for Sal's being hoisted atop the pizzeria. Spike wanted to keep it but it burned in the riot scene.

One of the murals specially painted for the film.

Facing page: WE LOVE Radio and "Mister Señor Love Daddy," Sam Jackson. When he's not on your radio, your radio really isn't on— "and that's the truth, Ruth."

Pages 86 and 87: "Tina," Rosie Perez, tearing it up in the opening credit dance sequence, "Fight the Power." The dance was choreographed by Rosie and Otis Sallid.

The corner men: "ML," Paul Benjamin; "Sweet Dick Willie," Robin Harris; and "Coconut Sid," Frankie Faison.

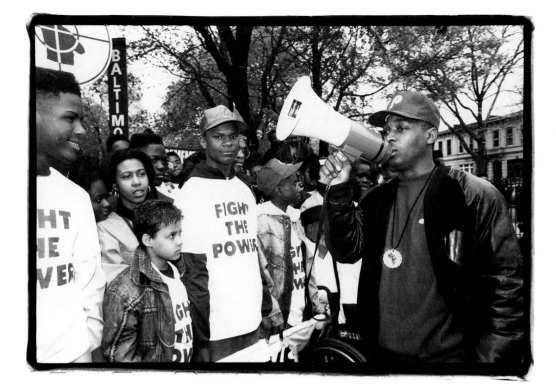

Danny Aiello, "Sal," and John Turturro, "Pino,"
kidding around.

Facing page: Spike staged a "March on Racism" with
Public Enemy for the "Fight the Power" music video.
The march was led by Chuck D, Flavor Flav, and
Terminator X of Public Enemy.

"Sal" and "Buggin' Out," Giancarlo Esposito.

Bottom: "Vito" (the cool white boy), Richard Edson. Spike saw Richard in the Jim Jarmusch film *Stranger Than Paradise* and wanted to work with him.

"Radio Raheem" (Mr. Love and Hate), Bill Nunn.

"Smiley," Roger Smith. This character was greatly influenced by
August Wilson's character "Gabriel" in *Fences* (played by Frankie Faison).

"Mother Sister," Ruby Dee. "If I can have half a marriage
like Ossie and Ruby do, I'll be lucky," Spike comments.

Facing page: "Da Mayor," Ossie Davis. Spike wrote him
as a Morehouse freshman saying that one day he would
direct him and Ruby Dee in a movie. *Jungle Fever*
was their third film together.

"Jade," Joie Lee, takes a break.

"Clifton," John Savage, sports the jersey of the
Great White Hope, Larry Bird.

**The Wall of Fame. Sal says, "This is my pizzeria.
Only American Italians on the wall."**

PINO: You gold-teeth, gold-chain-wearing, fried-chicken-and-biscuit-eatin', monkey, ape, baboon, big thigh, fast-running, three-hundred-sixty-degree-basketball-dunking spade, Moulan Yan, take ya slice a pizza and go the fuck back to Africa.

KOREAN CLERK: It's cheap, I got good price for you, Mayor Koch, "How I'm doing," chocolate-egg-cream-drinking, bagel and lox, B'nai Brith asshole.

MOOKIE: You Dago, Wop, garlic-breath, guinea, pizza-
slinging, spaghetti-bending, Vic Damone, Perry Como,
Luciano Pavarotti, Sole Mio, nonsinging motherfucker.

**"Ahmad," Steve White; "Cee," Martin Lawrence; "Ella,"
Christa Rivers; and "Punchy," Leonard Thomas.**

Facing page: Rosie and Spike waiting
for lighting adjustments.

Pages 100 and 101: Spike playing
da platters dat matter on
WE LOVE Radio.

Jade combs Mother Sister's hair.

Johnny pump.

"Charlie," Frank Vincent, gets soaked.

**Radio Raheem, Smiley, and Buggin' Out pay their
respects to Sal's Famous Pizzeria.**

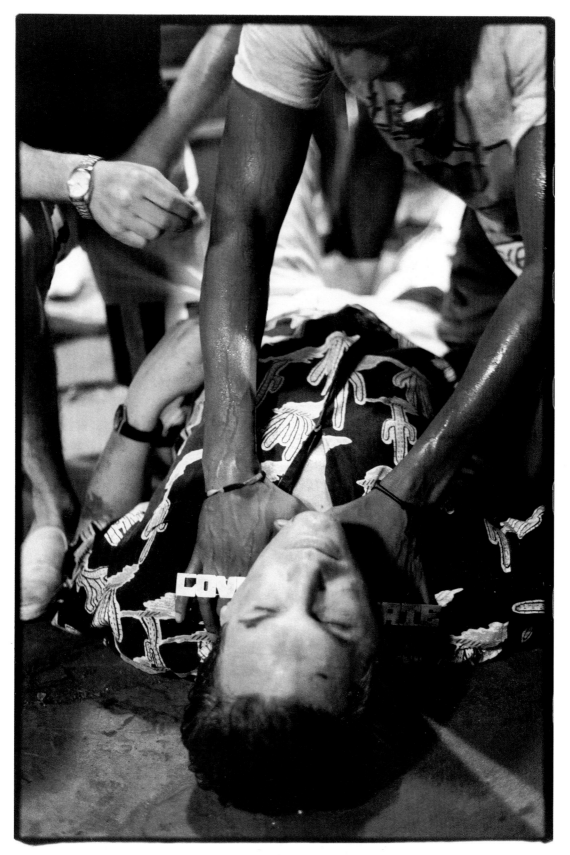

Sal gets choked.

**Rehearsing the New York Police Department
Michael Stewart choke hold.**

Murder by New York's Finest.

The calm before the storm.

Facing page: Practicing throwing garbage cans.

**Pages 108 and 109: Birmingham, Alabama,
or Brooklyn, New York.**

Mother Sister.

The fire this time.

The morning after.

Showdown at the O.K. Corral.

This plaque was put into the sidewalk on Stuyvesant
Street between Quincy Street and Lexington Avenue,
but a few months later someone dug it out of the
cement and stole it.

The crew of *Do the Right Thing*.

ONE MEANING OF MO' BETTER BLUES

CHARLES JOHNSON

TWO concepts—the "new Negro" and cultural nationalism—must be understood if we wish to unlock the artistic logic behind Spike Lee's fourth film, *Mo' Better Blues* (1990), and understand the position he has taken as a pro-black film director. Both concepts come from black people, one from Alain Locke, the Harlem Renaissance critic, and the other from the more important theoreticians of the black arts movement in the late 1960s.

In his essay "The New Negro" (1925), Locke describes the emergence of a new black art after World War I, a creative explosion brought about by a unique ensemble of social changes. The most important of these occurred when southern blacks fled racial violence and Jim Crow in the South by traveling to northern cities like New York's Harlem, where they interacted with Africans, West Indians, blacks free since the founding of the republic, and liberals—many of Jewish descent—fascinated, during the Roaring Twenties, with black folkways. All the elements were present, in this new black cauldron, for the creation of a progressive, international black consciousness and culture, and it was Locke who attempted to identify the new forms of black life emerging from the old. "The day of 'aunties,' 'uncles,' and 'mammies' is equally gone," he wrote. "Uncle Tom and Sambo have passed on. . . . In the very process of being transported the Negro is being transformed." One important feature of this new Negro of the 1920s, he said, was the appropriation by writers like Langston Hughes, Jean Toomer, and Zora Neale Hurston of hitherto unrecorded black folk sources for artistic inspiration. In the work of many Renaissance writers it was the everyday life of the ordinary black man and woman—our mothers and fathers, kin and friends—whom few (if any) white artists could depict, that became the subject of exploration and celebration.

For all the outpouring of creativity during the Harlem Renaissance, however, two forces brought the movement to an end—or to a forty-year interruption, if we consider the 1960s (and later the 1980s) to be its continuation, as many critics argue. One force was, as one might expect, the Great Depression. The other was a fickleness by the movement's white patrons, such as arts promoter and novelist Carl Van Vechten, who encouraged the Renaissance writers because they considered the Negro to be an exotic creature free of white men's cares and hang-ups—in other words, the patrons' sense of black life was as one-dimensional as that of earlier writers during the Joel Chandler Harris plantation school era. Not until the 1960s would we see a broad-based return by black artists to the pivotal theme of the Renaissance—the celebration of the folk—and by then it would assume a more political, Pan-Africanist form.

Black theoreticians of the black arts movement, the cultural wing of the black power movement, not only encouraged a return to the celebration of the common folk, but also emphasized the importance of the artists' sense of *community*. Authors such as Amiri Baraka (LeRoi Jones), the late Larry Neal, the late John Oliver Killens, and Gwendolyn Brooks expressed their belief that black artists—and especially the black musician—are the servants of their people, men and women who spring from the folk, draw their inspiration from them, and, most important, *return* to them for spiritual renewal. This cultural nationalist concept influenced an entire generation of young black creators. It's easy to see how this concept differs from the romantic tradition of the late nineteenth century, in which the artist is often portrayed as standing *separate* from his community—a genius or freak torn by his lonely talent from the context of family and friends. In this tradition, and in the films and books influenced by it, such as the film *Amadeus* and the Herman Hesse novel *Narcissus and Goldmund,* only the artist can hear the Muses; only he, like one of Plato's philosopher-kings in *The Republic,* sees clearly the essential forms of the world (recall the remark, in *Mo' Better Blues,* made sarcastically by would-be singer Clarke when her lover Bleek Gilliam is too absorbed in his music to even hear her: "Let me leave the artist at work alone. The muse is visiting and Bleek is truly inspired. Then he will share his newest, latest gift to the world. Hallelujah'').

Unlike the lonely artist of the Western romantic tradition, the cultural nationalist creator was seen as being *of* his people, and the highest regard was given to the men who produced jazz. Check out Henry Dumas's short story, "Will the Circle Be Unbroken?" (1966), in which the musician Probe plays music so anchored to the black world that it kills white members in the audience. The jazz-man, according to some 1960s critics, plays *with* others, and his work is a product of improvisation and spontaneity. If music is a "thing" in the Western tradition, fixed and made permanent by a text, in the black world it is deliberately short-lived, something that is mindful of its mortality, of the brief time that we have on this earth together: a music that happens at *this* moment only (if not recorded) and arises from the special interplay and dialectic of the jazz-man, his brothers on stage, and the audience *that* night. Black art, therefore, was seen as a We-relation. Such modern artists as John Coltrane (the guiding spirit of *Mo' Better*), Sonny Rollins, and Sun Ra were figures to emulate for the artists of the 1960s.

And so we come to the work of Spike Lee.

From his first film, *She's Gotta Have It* (1986), to *School Daze* (1988), to the highly controversial (and commercially successful) *Do the Right Thing* (1989), Mr. Lee reveals himself to be a director-writer-actor influenced by the principal thinkers of the black arts movement. He is, he says, a filmmaker who makes movies for black people (a position taken by poets like Neal and Baraka in their writing twenty-five years ago)—movies intended to counteract the negative and racist stereotyping of blacks found in films stretching from *Birth of a Nation* (1915) to the recent *Mississippi Burning* (1988). He is not, of course, our first black filmmaker, but in contrast to recent directors like Gordon Parks, Melvin Van Peebles, and the prolific Stan Lathan, he has established a style—part nationalist, part whimsy—that is clearly his own. In his films the *texture* of everyday black life is center stage—the feelings, rhythms, and unique panache of the common (black) man and woman are given full play. He achieves this, in part, by giving talented entertainers like the late Robin Harris, as comic Butterbean in *Mo' Better,* a great deal of latitude in bringing their own material to the set and, in part, by introducing memorable moments and flashes—the series of black men hitting on women in *She's Gotta Have It,* the three laid-back brothers signifying on the Korean fruit-and-vegetable stand in *Do the Right Thing,* the encounter between street bloods and college students at a Kentucky Fried Chicken in *School Daze,* and the band members ragging the perpetually late Left Hand Lacey about his French (white) girlfriend in *Mo' Better.* These moments come about because Mr. Lee listens, and listens extremely well, to what the folk are saying when they don't think anyone is watching them. For example, the scene in which the band members rag Left Hand Lacey has more the feel of being "caught" than planned; the actors, once they start to roll, step on one another's lines as in a real conversation, their joviality and ease as unmannered (and undirected) as if they were longtime buddies playing to a camcorder or to a hidden Candid Camera during a party.

Mr. Lee's films are built on these moments, not on Aristotelian dramatic principles. His approach, if I'm not mistaken, is to let textural moments of black life *happen* when he makes a motion picture, to let them accumulate slowly, so that by the film's end we have not so much the pleasant exhaustion that comes from a movie that propels us from the first frame to the last (as does any George Lucas film) but instead a collection of strong, black images and voices in our head when we leave the theater.

Few movie reviewers I read were kind to *Mo' Better Blues*. Inevitably, they drew comparisons—as did Mr. Lee himself—to other films about black musicians, specifically to *Round Midnight* (1986) and *Bird* (1988). In the companion volume to the film, *Mo' Better Blues* (New York: Simon & Schuster, 1990), Mr. Lee criticized both films for being "narrow depictions of the lives of Black musicians as seen through the eyes of White screenwriters and White directors. Two of the main characters in *Bird* are White. And of all the accounts of [Charlie] Parker's life that [Clint] Eastwood could have based his film on, he chose a book written by Bird's White wife, Chan Parker" (p. 39). Once he read that Woody Allen was also planning a film on jazz, Mr. Lee, the son of an accomplished bass player who has scored all his pictures, felt an even greater sense of urgency in portraying this subject from a black point of view. "You know I couldn't let Woody Allen do a jazz film before I did. I was on a mission."

Thus, he sets his fourth film—a work inspired by the black writer's determination to set the record straight—in 1969, when young Bleek Gilliam is ordered by his mother, Lillian, to continue practicing his trumpet when his friends arrive on their Brooklyn doorstep and want him to play:

LILLIAN: Bleek, didn't I tell you to tell your hoodlum friends not to come around here?
BIG STOP: Aw, Gem! Leave the boy alone.
BLEEK: Can I go outside now?
LILLIAN: Not until you finish your practice.
BLEEK: What about then?
LILLIAN: We'll see.
BIG STOP: Let the boy be a boy, have some fun.
LILLIAN: He could be a bum for all you care. Running the streets with those wild kids.

Lillian Gilliam (Abbey Lincoln) seems, to my eye, unnecessarily harsh and one-dimensional. Why, for example, is she so lacking in sympathy and only Bleek's father, Big Stop (Dick Anthony Williams), able to understand a child's desire to be with his friends? Although her shrillness mars this scene, the child actor, Zakee Howze, who plays Bleek, shows spunk and spirit when he shouts back at his friends that his practice time is important, then confides to his parents:

BLEEK: Mommy, I never get to play with my friends. Now they call me a sissy. I ain't no sissy.
LILLIAN: Don't pay those fools no mind.

BIG STOP: A SISSY!

BLEEK: I'm sick and tired of this trumpet. I hate the trumpet.

(Big Stop looks at his son, gets up from in front of the TV, and goes to him.)

BIG STOP: Don't say that, Bleek. You'll have a lot of time to play with your friends. Don't hate that instrument; it's also your friend. We'll go to a ballgame. Just you and me. I'll make it up to you.

(CLOSE—BLEEK)

BLEEK: I still hate it.

(Bleek sticks the trumpet into his mouth.)

Much like young Charles Foster Kane, pulled away from his sled in *Citizen Kane,* Bleek Gilliam seems at first to resent the future planned for him by an insensitive grown-up. Whether he has true musical genius or progresses in his craft through sheer doggedness and dint of will is something we're never told. Unlike Milos Forman, who developed the character of Mozart in *Amadeus,* Mr. Lee does not provide us with material that helps us gauge the talent of his musician. In *Amadeus,* we see Mozart not only memorize another musician's composition after hearing it only once but effortlessly improve on it right before the other man's eyes; we hear him re-create the style and sound of other artists at a party for the entertainment of his friends; and, finally, we watch him produce first drafts of operas that seem flawless, even on his deathbed, where he dictates to a lesser artist a masterpiece that has the baffled scribe shouting, "Wait! What's that? You're going too fast!" These are, just maybe, the earmarks of musical genius, of a God-given talent so great, so mysterious it nearly tears apart the (Western) artist, who is always at pains to control these demons that whisper to him in a language of beauty and light few others can hear. Is Bleek so torn? We don't have enough insight into him to say. Yet it's clear that he *does* learn his mother's lesson about being dedicated to music and that during this learning process he also develops a staggering sense of self-regard and a selfishness that lay the foundation for the conflicts he will have twenty years later in his life—which Mr. Lee "smash-cuts" to, covering two decades of potential character development in the blink of an eye—with another musician in his band, Shadow Henderson (Wesley Snipes), his two lovers, Clarke (Cynda Williams) and Indigo (Joie Lee), and his manager, Giant, played by Mr. Lee himself.

The world of Bleek Gilliam, played as an adult by heartthrob Denzel Washington, centers on the smoky, below-ground *Beneath the Underdog* (the title refers to Charles Mingus's autobiography), an incongruously spacious nightclub (since it's in a basement) built in the late 1930s and usually packed with, as its name and design suggest, New York City's underdogs. In effect, the nightclub is a stage for Bleek's ego. It is *his* band, and no one else is allowed to perform original music. Giant, a gambler who can't get the group a better contract, often enrages the other artists, but he is Bleek's childhood friend since the third grade and, therefore, won't be replaced. And, perhaps worst of all, Bleek refuses to give Clarke the break she needs as a singer to make it in show business. Mr. Lee creates, as a backdrop for Bleek, a world of hauntingly beautiful music, of black performers who imitate the dress of their idols from decades past and look *good* on stage, of admiring women as different as Clarke and Indigo (a schoolteacher), and of white club owners—Moe and Josh Flatbush (John and Nicholas Turturro)—who exploit black talent. And within the band itself, Mr. Lee creates competition among other artists who feel they have not received the recognition that is their due. In *Mo' Better Blues,* the formidable antagonist is Shadow, who provides, I believe, a charismatic depiction of a talented, "overshadowed" black man who, by turns, can be sinister then consoling, crisply intelligent then goofy (the scene in which he talks about condoms with Giant), coolly professional then hot tempered. Shadow, in short, is unpredictable, and we watch him closely whenever he enters and threatens to take over a scene. One of Bleek's problems is that he doesn't watch Shadow enough.

During their sets, Shadow plays grandstanding solos that, according to Bleek, take "all day and night." It is Shadow who, potentially, can take it all away from Bleek—his band, his woman. Their differences are highlighted when, at a party, Bleek gives vent to his frustration as a black artist:

> BLEEK: I'm convinced Black folks are ignorant. We just plain are. I'm sick and tired of playing before everybody but my own people. They don't come out. We don't support our own. If Black artists, if I had to rely on niggers to eat, I'd starve to death. Jazz is our music, but we don't support it. It's sad, but true.
> SHADOW: Bleek, you're fulla shit. People like what they like. If grandiose motherfuckers like you presented the music in a way that they like it, motherfuckers would come.
> BLEEK: Oh yeah!
> SHADOW: Yeah! That's the way I'm gonna do it. Black folks will come. You watch.

I wondered how to interpret this exchange. On one level, Bleek is articulating the frustration many musicians feel when jazz is such a rage with whites and lately with Asians, yet responded to with indifference by many African-Americans, especially of the last generation. (Perhaps *Round Midnight* didn't get this entirely wrong.) But because these words come from Bleek, they reveal something about the inner discomfort he has felt since childhood toward his craft. No such friction between artist and audience seems to apply to Shadow, whose only goal appears to be providing others (including Clarke) with whatever brings them pleasure. We tend to agree with him when he says, "All Bleek cares about is Bleek." Shadow's evaluation of Bleek is especially harsh when it's clear that the band's leader won't give Clarke a shot at singing with the quintet: "Anything that might overshadow him, he blocks, like myself. I should be leader of this motherfucker, not Bleek."

But despite these professional conflicts in the life of Bleek Gilliam, and despite Mr. Lee's statement that "I always knew I would do a movie about music," the plot of *Mo' Better Blues* unfolds less in the direction of an artist's struggle with his craft (or his audience) than as a love triangle. "This time out," Mr. Lee said, "I chose to explore male-female relationships. All artists are driven by love for their art, and great artists are selfish in their devotion to it." He continued:

> This is Bleek Gilliam to a T. His music is his number one. So where do the women (two) in his life fit in? How do Clarke and Indigo deal with the fact that he is seeing both of them at the same time? And how does he tell them that they will always be second fiddle to his trumpet? That's some cold shit, and it takes a strong woman to stay with a man like that (p. 31).

To a great extent, then, *Mo' Better Blues* is a movie thematically at war with itself, alternating from the goal of addressing a black musician's life from a black perspective to dwelling on the sex life of Bleek Gilliam. As things turn out, the love story wins out, claiming more dramatic time in the movie than the tale of the artist's life.

There are scenes with Bleek making love to Clarke, Shadow doing the do with Clarke, and Bleek and Indigo engaging in foreplay, which takes the form of the artist pretending to be Dracula descending, his cape fluttering, on his latest victim. Once the story settles into this direction, *Mo' Better Blues* doesn't return to the initial question raised about the relationship of the musician to his craft. Instead, Bleek Gilliam's energy is consumed by the dilemma of having both Clarke and Indigo turn up at the club on the same night wearing identical dresses he bought for them in Paris. As Bleek tries to maintain his relationship with these women, he finds himself calling Clarke by Indigo's name (and vice versa) and mistaking one woman for the other during the act of making love—the contours of the women's individual lives blurring before his eyes as the two romances unravel, Clarke opting to fall in with Shadow and Indigo finally washing her hands of Bleek altogether. He has a shoving match with Shadow after Giant informs him that his chief competitor is boning Clarke. But it is not this conflict that Mr. Lee chooses for Bleek's ultimate demise. No, the coup de grace is provided by the worsening gambling debts incurred by Giant and by the loyalty of Bleek to his old friend.

Mr. Lee gives himself, as Woody Allen might, the role of comic foil for the other actors. Although he is called Giant, Shadow refers to him as midget and, in the movie's most devastating example of the Dozens, berates his work as manager (and his size) by remarking, "You keep coming up *short*." Which is true, for as a gambler, Giant is losing big. While biking one afternoon, he is pulled into a car by two thugs, Rod (Leonard Thomas) and Madlock (Samuel L. Jackson), who tell him, "We don't believe in killing our brothers and sisters," then proceed to break the fingers on Giant's left hand. Mr. Lee gives these two sinister gangsters a touch of self-mockery. They pursue Giant to the nightclub on the very night Bleek has promised to help pay off his gambling debts, and drag him outside into an alley for another beating. When Bleek intervenes to help Giant, Madlock busts him full in his face with his trumpet, effectively bringing the musician's career to an end.

If Madlock and Rod are portrayed as caricatures of criminal types, the same must be said of other, secondary characters in *Mo' Better Blues*. Mr. Lee enjoys presenting them in pairs: the black bouncers Eggy and Born Knowledge (the latter breaks into a rap about the Black Man being God that at first glance might please many cultural nationalists, then make them knit their brows when they realize how they've been lampooned). And in yet another comic pairing, which led to some controversy for the film, we have the club owners Josh and Moe. When we are first introduced to these entrepreneurs, who inherited Beneath the Underdog from their father, they are singing praises to money—how numbers will never let you down, how you can count (literally) on the unwavering certainty of digits (a cash register ringing, say) more than you can on other people. For some critics, Josh and Moe are stereotypes of Jewish people whose presence is so widely felt in the entertainment business. A viewer must admit that they are offered to us in one dimension only, not as sympathetically rendered characters (for example, as Clarke is presented) but as clones of one another, making identical gestures at the same moment and completing each other's sentences as if they were Siamese twins, or two halves of the same person. They refuse to renegotiate the contract for the Bleek Quintet after the band becomes one of the club's hottest acts; Moe threatens, with a laugh, to sue Bleek if he tries to take his band elsewhere, and after Giant and Bleek take the beating of their lives in the alley, Moe tries to convince Shadow and the other musicians to go back inside and play. (Shadow refuses, swearing never to work for them again.) Nowhere does Mr. Lee say the Flatbush brothers are Jewish, but a few cultural eccentricities associated with the stereotype of Jewish businessmen are clearly present in these portrayals. A viewer is forced to conclude that, unlike Eggy and Born Knowledge (a lampoon of an idea), these comic club owners (a lampoon of an ethnic group) are less successful—and just maybe offensive to black and white audiences alike.

After the alleyway beating, Bleek Gilliam goes into hiding for a year. He is visited in the hospital by Big Stop. Back in his loft, which looks as if a tornado has passed through, he heals slowly and, apparently, reflects on the errors he's made that transformed his talent from a blessing into a curse and drove away the people closest to him. A full year passes before Giant, now working as a doorman and taking self-help classes to cure his gambling, sees Bleek again, this time on the street outside the Dizzy Club, which is featuring the Shadow Henderson Quartet, with Clarke as its singer. We learn that old wounds have healed. Former adversaries—and hurt lovers—are capable of forgiveness. Shadow has invited Bleek to sit in with his new band. As Bleek enters the nightclub, he is greeted warmly by applause. These people *do* care about him, no matter how badly he'd behaved in the past. Clarke gives him a kiss. No question she will remain with Shadow; the tenderness in her kiss suggests that you don't have to make love to everyone you love. The other musicians embrace Bleek, welcoming him back from the exile to which he was condemned by his own ego. Sadly, though, when he begins to play it's clear to everyone, most of all Bleek, that he's lost his gift. The gods, you might say, have taken it back because he abused it, and there's no sense in his trying to fool himself. Quietly, he—a figure of tragedy—leaves the stage and strides past the audience and then out onto the street, with Giant chasing behind him. "I'll never play again," he says, handing his trumpet to his oldest friend. Giant shouts at him as his figure recedes in the rain, "I won't sell it!"

The next scene occurs when Bleek, sopping wet, turns up at Indigo's apartment. Naturally, she's furious that she hasn't heard from him in over a year. But by now Bleek is not "too proud to beg" for her love.

> BLEEK: You gotta let me redeem myself.
> INDIGO: Redemption. The only reason you're here is because you can't play anymore and Clarke is with Shadow,.
> (He puts his hands on Indigo's shoulders.)
> INDIGO: Don't, Bleek.
> BLEEK: I once read, I forget where, a married couple was on a plane and it was going down into the sea. Without thinking, they tore off their clothes and began to make love ferociously, right there in their seats, oblivious to anyone and everything. They didn't care. The plane was about to crash and they all would be dead.
> INDIGO: Get off me, Bleek.
> BLEEK: They loved each other dearly and wanted to be together if they had to go. That plane, by some miracle, avoided crashing, but how were they to know?
> (Bleek is now pressed up against Indigo as she struggles.)

Bleek's anecdote here, delivered at a crucial moment in a pivotal scene, is misleading. It says that in order "to be together" the couple on the airplane have to strip and start screwing. If I understand Bleek's story to Indigo, they are *already* together on the plane. By choosing this story to tell, the musician suggests, I'm afraid, that intercourse is the only way for two people to express their genuine devotion to each other. Nevertheless, the anecdote and his sincerity have the desired effect on Indigo. They make love, not the "mo' better" sort of sex after which the movie is named, not a simple "dick thing," as Bleek called his earlier affairs, but instead a surrender to each other. For Bleek, it is also a surrender of himself to others, a return to the world of the folk and family. In his script for *Mo' Better,* Mr. Lee writes that the end of the film was to be exactly seven minutes and forty-six seconds, which is the length of John Coltrane's "A Love Supreme." That composition plays over the montage that covers the next eight years in the life of Bleek and Indigo: their marriage, the day a son is born to them, the happy parents taking their child to an apartment in Brooklyn; the boy (named Miles) growing up; and Miles practicing the trumpet as Bleek himself had done in 1969. The budding musician's friends come to the house, shouting for him to come down and play. Indigo, now in the role of Lillian, says Miles must finish practicing first. We have cycled back to the movie's exact beginning—a contrivance to be sure, and the dialogue is the same, but with one difference. Bleek tells his wife, "Let the boy have some fun." Together in the window, with Indigo leaning into her husband, whose face registers a quiet maturity and peace we haven't seen before, they watch Miles race off, enjoying the freedom of childhood that Bleek was denied.

In *Mo' Better Blues* we end where we begin, with the black family. The life of the black artist is saved, Mr. Lee seems to be saying, by friends and kin—by Coltrane's sense of a love supreme—when his talent is lost and he has no refuge other than the family to restore his dignity. It is a movie that emphasizes the social side of the artist's life, a life with others, as black arts movement theoreticians urged us to embrace in the very year—1969—the movie opens. No one can deny that there are technical and thematic problems galore in Mr. Lee's fourth outing as a filmmaker. It is far too loose in structure to generate suspense. It needs, in nearly every scene, more attention to character. Although it is a far quieter and gentler film than *Do the Right Thing,* at its heart is the love-triangle idea that formed the basis of *She's Gotta Have It,* but in that movie the central theme does not have to compete with a host of other issues ranging from the exploitation of black creativity to replacing white images of black musicians with black ones. And, personally, I object to the notion that "great artists are selfish in their devotion" to their art, because we have too many examples of artists of the first rank who did not sacrifice their family lives, fidelity to their spouses, and loyalty to their friends to create beauty—authors such as Wallace Stevens and Ralph Ellison leap immediately to mind.

But the thought that Mr. Lee has used as a thread through this picture has a meaning every black artist—musician, painter, actor, or writer—knows only too well if he has plied his trade in the world and come wearily back home, not as a celebrated creator, just as a homeboy hoping to draw strength from those who love him even if he fails, even if his talent flees, even if he has nowhere else to turn. That meaning in *Mo' Better Blues* does not leave us: *You can't do it alone.* And, more important, *You don't have to.*

"Bleek Gilliam," Denzel Washington.

Bleek and Indigo.

Facing page: Love triangle.

"Clarke Bentancourt," Cynda Williams.

"Indigo Downes," Joie Lee.

"Left Hand Lacey," Giancarlo Esposito.

"Giant" (the world's worst manager but ya gotta love him), Spike Lee.

The Bleek Gilliam Quintet (left to right): "Rhythm
Jones," Jeff 'Tain' Watts; "Left Hand Lacey"; "Bleek";
"Shadow Henderson," Wesley Snipes; and
"Bottom Hammer," Bill Nunn.

Pages 132 and 133: "Bleek" may look like Miles, but the
only real musician in the Bleek Gilliam Quintet
was "Rhythm"—Jeff Watts.

Raymond Jones put a new melody to W. C. Handy's "Harlem Blues."
Here he's going over it in the studio with Cynda Williams.

"Denzel, let's try it this way, maybe."

Facing page: Posters blown up from the cover of John Coltrane's album
A Love Supreme were placed throughout the set.

Bleek and that damn red dress.

Bleek and that damn red dress again.

**Production designer Wynn Thomas's baby, the
Beneath the Underdog club.**

**The trumpet rarely left Denzel's hand, both on and off
the set.**

"Butterbean Jones," played by the late, great comic,
Robin Harris. Robin passed away before the film
was finished.

Facing page: Bleek and Shadow, both talented but with
different views on music.

It started to rain during
this scene as Rhythm Jones
and Bottom Hammer
walk to the gig.

Giant is a born loser. Everybody can see this but Bleek.

**Even though *Mo' Better Blues* takes place in the present
day, the musicians dress like the cats did in the be-bop
era, a homage to their heroes.**

Pages 146 and 147: Solo on the Brooklyn Bridge.

The Turturro brothers, "Josh and Moe Flatbush."
Why are these guys smiling and not Bleek?
Ever heard of Morris Levy?

Giant and Bleek reunited.

Facing page: Spike did all his own stunts.

Pages 150 and 151: Clarke interrupts practice.

Giant takes it on the chin.

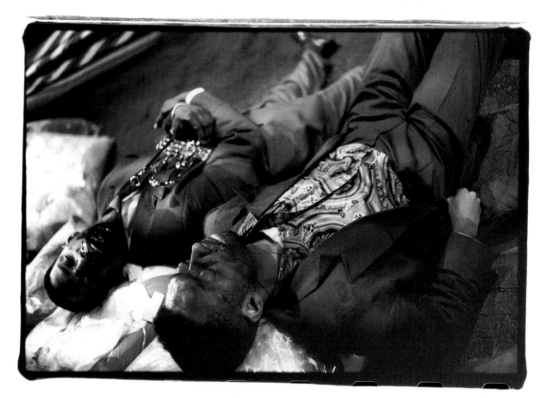

Giant and Bleek, beaten to a pulp.

Nervous breakdown.

The rooftop wedding of Bleek and Jade.

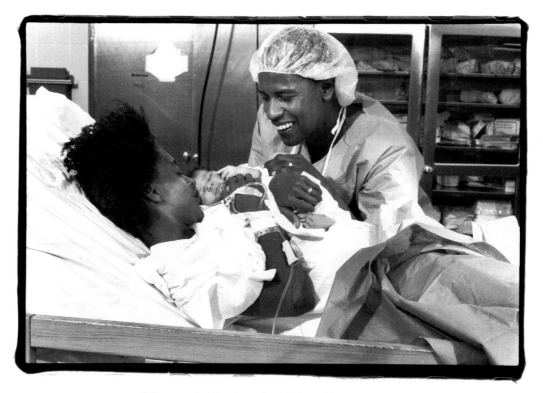

Spike actually filmed two live births at Harlem Hospital,
and he's a godfather.

Gilliam family portrait.

Five-year-old "Miles Gilliam," Zakee L. Howze, wants to
go out and play just like his father did at that age.

"Giant" with his main man, "Petey," Rubén Blades.

Facing page, top, left to right: Bill Lee, Spike,
Branford Marsalis, Kenny Kirkland, Jeff Watts, and
Terence Blanchard going over changes in the number
for the Bleek Gilliam Quintet.

Facing page, bottom: Terence Blanchard, creating the
sound of Bleek as Bill Lee looks on.

**Left to right: Ernest Dickerson, cameraman; Robi Reed,
casting; Monty Ross, co-producer; Wynn Thomas,
production design; and Jon Kilik, line producer.**

The cast.

JUNGLE FEVER

JUNGLE FEVER; OR, GUESS WHO'S NOT COMING TO DINNER?

HENRY LOUIS GATES, JR.

I would not have believed it unless I had been there. I was sitting at Forty Acres and a Mule Filmworks, Spike Lee's offices in Brooklyn, waiting for a taxi to take me back to Manhattan. The morning had been spent with Spike Lee and two editors, watching the rough cut of his fifth film, *Jungle Fever,* subtitled appropriately, *From Harlem to Bensonhurst and BACK*!

As we sat together, talking about the pleasures of working with Ruby Dee and Ossie Davis, in walked a white actress who had worked with Lee on *Jungle Fever.* She began by talking about her recent experiences in Hollywood, then, abruptly, launched into a monologue about interracial dating—about her severe reservations about it. She stated flatly that although she didn't mind it for other people, she could never imagine having such a relationship.

As I sat there, dumbfounded, wondering whether she was putting us on—wondering, indeed, as I had been throughout the screening, if *any* intelligent human being in the late twentieth century could allow race, creed, or national origin to determine the selection of a lover—this actress paused, reflected a bit, then confessed that she *had* met a tall Nigerian on the plane from LA, she *had* found him attractive, he *had* once dated a French woman ("So he *does* date white girls"), and she *had* asked him to give her a call. "Zulu dick," Spike and I said simultaneously as we burst into laughter, referring to one of the signal sexual myths about men of African descent that *Jungle Fever* seeks to examine and critique.

Honest and open explorations of the complexities of interracial sexual attraction have not been among Hollywood's strong points. Black-white sexual attraction has been treated as bestial and demeaning, as it was in *Birth of a Nation* (1915), where the fondest wish of the newly emancipated slave, D. W. Griffith argued frame after frame, was to rape a white woman. It has been portrayed as lurid and titillating, as in *Shaft* (1971), where the eponymous hero makes love to a prostitute in his shower, or as in *100 Rifles* (1969), where Jim Brown makes wild and passionate love to Raquel Welch, cast as a leader of an Indian rebellion. Or else it has been almost completely sublimated, and here Sidney Poitier made a small fortune as Sublimation Man, first in *A Patch of Blue* (1965), where a blind girl falls in love unwittingly with a quite brown Poitier, and then in *Guess Who's Coming to Dinner?* (1967), where Katherine Houghton reveals to her mother, played by Katharine Hepburn, that she and Sidney have not yet made love "because he wouldn't let me!" Even I, sixteen-year-old West Virginia country boy that I was when I saw the film, knew *that* line was a lie.

But *Guess Who's Coming to Dinner?* presented a significant theme of the civil rights movement. A paragon of the race, Sidney Poitier is not only a doctor but a potential candidate for the Nobel Prize in medicine. He has been educated in and taught at America's finest universities, he is self-effacing ("How have you achieved so *much* so quickly?" Spencer Tracy asks him; "White people have treated me so well to show that they aren't prejudiced," he responds with a straight face), and he is honest (who can forget that he asks the operator for time and charges when he phones his folks long distance in Tracy's study, then leaves the *exact* change in a neatly stacked pile smack dab in the middle of Tracy's desk!). Now that is one bad brother, I remember thinking when I first saw the film. (I decided to go to medical school right then and there.) But the point, of course, was that he wasn't bad at all: he was the perfect Un-Negro, with a PhD and MD in hand, stocking-capped with closely cropped hair, and a voice showing no trace of the plantation or the ghetto. This film, ironically, did more to fuel the death of the civil rights movement and the birth of black nationalism than did any other film because it suggested that the movement would achieve its fulfillment in the creation of a new middle class—assimilated, desexualized, and safe. (The sole "sexual" contact between the lead characters is one passionless American kiss, revealed to viewers through the mediation of a taxi's rear-view mirror.)

It's safe to say that the frisson of miscegenation has never been treated in American film with either intelligence or candor. Until now.

Jungle Fever is a film that explores the racial stereotypes and sexual taboos that Western culture, in general, and American society, in particular, have found endlessly fascinating almost since the first day that the European encountered the "black other" many centuries ago. It also gives evidence of how these stereotypes and taboos have become reinforced by social or class stratifications. (But it is also a film about intrablack sexuality—healthy, loving, generously amusing sexuality between black people who love each other—and this very well might be one of the film's most profound contributions to black cultural expression.) Although most critics have somehow missed this crucial aspect of Lee's oeuvre, few contemporary creative artists in any medium have taken greater pains to depict the way that categories such as class and race subtend each other in American racial relations. We see this in *Do the Right Thing*, especially in the exchanges among the three men on the street— the filmic equivalent of the Greek chorus in classical Greek drama—and in the "talking heads" scene in which representatives of different hyphenated-American ethnic types take turns insulting their less favorite "other," often using interchangeable ethnic slurs and stereotypical racist structures. In *Jungle Fever*, Lee deftly establishes the economic foundation of racism, on which white Western xenophobia has constructed an entire metaphysics of black sexuality, by *reversing* our normal expectations of the distribution of class status, educational background, and financial stability among the film's black and white characters.

Jungle Fever opens with a copy of *The New York Times* hitting the stoop of a gorgeous brownstone on Striver's Row, traditionally the nicest neighborhood in Harlem. Upstairs, a couple, Flipper and Drew Purify, are "making love like mad," as the script directs, while their ten-year-old daughter, Ming (Veronica Timbers), sits in bed, listening. Flipper (Wesley Snipes) is "blue black," and Drew (Lonette McKee) is what the tradition calls "lightskinned." Flipper and Drew are an ideal couple: in love, passionately; smart; successful in their careers; and financially secure. Flipper, we soon learn, is an architect, hoping soon to be made a partner, while Drew is a buyer at Bloomingdale's. At breakfast, Ming (who feigns sleep each morning when her father comes to wake her) engages her parents in the most honest and open discussion of sex between a child and her parents that I have seen in American film. Then Flipper walks Ming to school, in what is obviously as much a part of his daily ritual as is making love with Drew. Here we see drawn, most effectively, an ultimately stable black upper-middle-class family, the epitome of the race's social aspirations for over a hundred years. We know that this blissful existence, on the very street where W. E. B. DuBois lived in the 1920s, cannot be destined to last.

Flipper's office at the architectural firm of Mast and Covington introduces the central conflict of the film. Flipper's black secretary, Terri Niles (Cynda Williams), is moving to Chicago and getting married. "I love this," Flipper says, as he wanders alone and alienated at an office party on her behalf, "Black people in love." It soon becomes clear that Flipper's senior partners, Jerry and Leslie (Tim Robbins and Brad Dourif), have no intention of removing him from the indeterminate position he is in: the backbone of the firm, who has to work "like a Georgia mule," as he tells Terri, to prove that he is capable of being a partner. Jerry and Leslie rib Flipper about living in Harlem, telling him that he'll have to move once he becomes partner. When he responds that he'll move to Connecticut once he becomes a partner, Jerry makes a bad joke about them becoming neighbors, underscoring, again, the class distinction between them. Despite Flipper's and Drew's apparent success, then, it is clear that Flipper is vulnerable within the larger power structure.

The next day, Jerry and Leslie introduce Flipper to Angie Tucci (Annabella Sciorra), Terri's replacement as Flipper's secretary. "Tucci" is, of course, a pun on "tush," so we know that this spells trouble: "She's all yours," Leslie says when she's introduced. Flipper, in private, protests, repeating his stated preference for a black secretary, a protest that leads to a taunting exchange with his bosses about reverse discrimination.

Cut to Bensonhurst, the home of the working-class, uncultivated, ignorant, and racist Tucci family, headed by the head couch potato and racist Mike Tucci (Frank Vincent), and sons Charlie and Jimmy (David Dundara and Michael Imperioli), Mike's junior racists:

CHARLIE: I like the Mets now. Only two niggers on the whole squad.
JIMMY: Strawberry and Gooden. One's an ex-coke fiend, the other's an ex-alcoholic.
MIKE: The two number-one shines.

Brief flashes of dialogue such as these establish the working-class background, ethnic origins, and predispositions of these characters. Clearly the three would choke on their pasta if they knew the complexion of Angie's new boss.

The characters' exchanges establish the contrast in light and dark that runs throughout this movie like a leitmotif; indeed, dark and light symbolism plays back and forth in a highly patterned and beautifully layered chiaroscuro. Flipper, Drew, and Ming are the positive forces of the family unit; Mike, Charlie, and Jimmy Tucci are the resentful white ethnics of Bensonhurst, whose own sense of powerlessness as working-class types has killed most of their humanity and forced them, in turn, to find someone else to hate and (they hope) to exploit, in turn, just as they are exploited. Angie is the angel who possesses the sole spark of humanity in the Tucci household and whom her father and brothers exploit. She is, in fact, the nigger of the family. The Tucci household is the ugly double, the antithesis, of Flipper's.

Angie's longtime beau is Paulie Carbone (John Turturro), a sensitive, if ineffectual, young man whose first love is chess—and perhaps his regular chess partner, Herman Russo (Carl Capotorto). Angie and Paulie's relationship, it quickly becomes clear, is (and has always been) platonic. Paulie is the "sensitive other" of his neighborhood, who tends the newspaper-cum-soda-fountain candy store owned by his father, Lou (Anthony Quinn). Together, he and Angie cling to each other for light in the darkness of Bensonhurst.

Angie's oppression—her "niggering" by social, and more immediately, familial confines—is brought into bold relief in the next scene, at the home of Flipper's parents, the Good Reverend Doctor (Ossie Davis) and his wife, Lucinda Doctor (Ruby Dee). The Good Reverend Doctor is a (forcibly) retired minister who listens obsessively to Mahalia Jackson and seemingly searches the Bible for vivid passages naming sins of the flesh. We get the feeling that the Good Reverend Doctor has succumbed to this very temptation and has been put out to pasture because of it. Here we meet their oldest son, Gator (Sam Jackson), a crack addict, who represents Flipper's other self, the self that he escaped becoming. Gator visits to borrow money from his mom; later he'll "borrow" their color TV. In the Doctor family, Lee employs the use of archetypes, with the characters being more allegorical cultural types than individuals. This use of allegory, along with the use of talking heads addressing the camera, is an effective way to disrupt the realistic narrative frame in which many black films—and all the black visual and written arts—have been imprisoned and delimited. Lee's Brechtian deployment of archetypes gives his films the air of medieval morality tales brought splendidly up to date. But rather than being confined to any one simple level of signification (say, the enactment of ethnic conflict), his characters, and their conflicts, produce a multiplex of meaning.

When the Good Reverend Doctor announces to no one in particular that "the Devil's work is never done," that "the Devil is always busy," we know that Flipper and the devil's angel, Angie, are about to get down. Flipper and Angie's love scene is graphically rendered, the most passionate interracial sex scene that I can recall. (Flipper and Angie make Jim Brown and Raquel Welch look like a tea party with Jack and Jill.) Their tentative, then energetic, exploration of each other's bodies reads like the detailed and innocent charting by two explorers of a foreign and strangely exotic continent. An altogether believable magnetism is at work, as Angie confesses her attraction to the beauty of Flipper's very black skin. Exhausted and spent, Flipper lies across Angie's body to form a crucifix image, one draped in red, black, and green as the camera pans away. Flipper, we think, is a dead man.

Angie's sexual bonding with Flipper is contrasted with Paulie's odd relationship with his father, as the scene cuts to Paulie and Lou's bathroom, where Paulie draws Lou's bath, then washes his back. Again, a brilliantly succinct exchange *specifies* the nature of racism, with Lou sharing with his son his ingenious theory for the speed of black athletes: "They're from the jungle. They outrun lions and tigers. . . . How do you think they send messages? Some white guy in a jeep? *On foot!*" Had it not been for Jimmy the Greek and Al Campanis, several scenes such as these would have been hard for average Americans to believe.

Paulie heads off to their candy store, where he reads a book, in stark contrast to his friends and hangers-on, illiterate "pure D racists" from Bensonhurst. Paulie tells them the plot of the book he is reading—that five Sicilians in Louisiana owned a factory in 1890 and gave their black workers equal partnership. When their fellow white citizens learned the news, they lynched the Italians. Paulie's parable underscores what the film has been saying, implicitly, thus far: how very much economics is the foundation on which racism is built. As Vinny (Nick Turturro) responds, "Good. They got what they deserved. They shouldn't a got involved with no niggers in the first place." Enter Orin Goode (Tyra Ferrell), from a respectable black Bensonhurst family, asking Paulie when his father's going to start selling the *Times*.

It is clear that Paulie likes Orin and wishes to date her, much to the chagrin of his white and vulgar buddies, just as he likes Herman, his chess-playing buddy. Herman's attraction to Paulie makes his friends just as uncomfortable as does Paulie's attraction to Orin. The rampant homophobia of the white working class is Lee's theme here, and it is rendered with both poignancy and lightness of touch. (Two black gay men, the size of football players, will make a crucial appearance late in the film, defending Flipper and his best friend, Cyrus [Spike Lee], from Angie's irate brothers and their friends.)

Meanwhile, back at the firm, Flipper demands to be made a partner and, of course, is put off. He quits in a huff, intending to start his own architectural business. Seeking the solace of Cyrus, he confesses his unfaithfulness:

> CYRUS: I thought you were gonna drop a bomb.
> FLIPPER: She's WHITE!
> CYRUS: WHITE!
> FLIPPER: ITALIAN.
> CYRUS: H-BOMB.
> FLIPPER: From Bensonhurst.
> CYRUS: NUCLEAR MEGATON BOMB.

In a parallel scene, Angie confesses to her two girlfriends, Denise (Debi Mazar) and Louise (Gina Mastrogiacomo). In a hilarious scene, in which their talking heads face the camera, Angie's friends repeat virtually all the sexual stereotypes about black men that continue to reign supreme in American culture, from "big swallowing lips" to a foot-and-a-half-long penis, just as Cyrus repeats the standard stereotypes about white women ("Does she have a butt? No? She has a flat, white butt, right? She got TITTIES! At least some TITTIES.")

Once these revelations occur, we know that Flipper and Angie's privacy will be violated. Cyrus tells his wife, Vera (Veronica Webb), who of course tells her best friend, Drew. Angie's friends tell all of Bensonhurst. Drew throws Flipper's possessions into the street, and Angie is thrown out of her home: but not before fifteen "mouths" again utter all the stereotypes about interracial sex to the camera:

> MOUTH NO. 13: There is only one thing he could possibly want from her . . .
> MOUTH NO. 14: . . . that good white pussy.
> MOUTH NO. 15: . . . that good black dick.

One of the film's most compelling scenes is a "wake" held at Drew's apartment with several of her girlfriends, as they analyze Flipper's affair with Angie. Here, these black women talk about the pressures of education and class status on the selection of a lover, the scarcity of black men in their social and economic class, and the nature of their own sexual desires. This is a refreshingly open and revealing scene, the ultimate communal feminist moment in a major black film released to this time.

> NILDA: It's different. White men treat me like some exotic animal or something. I'm still looking for a strong black man to date.
> VERA: Good luck.

INEZ: I think there's a lot of self-hate when a black man doesn't want to deal with a sister.

ANGELA: But at the same time you still date white men.

INEZ: Yeah, but at the same time I also date black men. I've also dated Chinese, Latino, Jewish.

DREW: That ain't no consolation.

INEZ: I know you think I should only date black. But I'm gonna date who I like. Who's nice to me, who's sweet to me, who loves me.

DREW: Can't you find a black man to do that?

INEZ: Who should I date? Find me one. JUST ONE.

DREW: He's out there.

INEZ: Drew, if it will make you happy I'll make a pilgrimage to Africa, the Motherland, to find myself a true tribesman.

VERA: A true Asiatic black man.

INEZ: With a dick down to his knees. Keep me happy for days.

NILDA: That ZULU dick.

INEZ: I want me some Zulu dick in the bush.

(They all laugh.)

ANGELA: Do you know what it is like not being thought of as attractive? I was always the darkest one in my class. All the guys ran after the light-skin girls with long straight hair. That left me out. That same thinking leaves us out to white women. Back in the day brothers just got women that looked like Drew and Vera, now light skin ain't good enough. Today, brothers are going for the GUSTO, the real McCoy. That's why Flipper is gone. White girls got it made.

VERA: If I see Cyrus even glancing at a white woman I will kill him dead.

The intraracial color-as-class tensions that Lee parodied in *School Daze* are in this scene rendered in full and beautiful detail. In this communal, feminist sharing of traditional racial wisdom, the tensions brought on by race and class and by color and hair texture are revealed as never before in the history of film. This is a brilliantly created and executed scene, one destined to be analyzed and imitated, thank goodness, as black film continues to come of age in this decade.

The film ends with a reconciliation between Flipper and Drew, after Flipper and Cyrus have a journey to Bensonhurst in search of Angie, who has walked out on Flipper. Cyrus and Flipper escape their deaths (which we expect) only narrowly, saved by Cyrus's mad and unlicensed dash for freedom behind the driver's wheel.

Just as *Guess Who's Coming to Dinner?* was the civil rights era's film, par excellence, so, too, is *Jungle Fever* the film that most effectively serves as a vehicle for symbolizing both the marginality and the assimilation of the new, young, black, upper middle class: neo-nationalistic, thoroughly bourgeois, unsafe at any speed, and marvelously sexual. *Jungle Fever* is a subtle treatment of the complex nature of desire—both sexual and material—and the ramifications of an economic order that uses color distinctions (intraracial and interracial) and a racist mythology constructed around those color distinctions to cement social stratification. What is most striking to me is how many new themes Lee manages to sound in what could have easily become a one-dimensional melodrama about a quick-and-sordid love affair between an upper-middle-class black architect and his working-class white secretary. As few filmmakers have managed, Lee combines a sense of humor with larger political concerns: his vision is both playful and serious.

Jungle Fever shows how overdetermined interracial contact is in American society—overdetermined by hundreds of years of exploitation, mythology, and pseudoscience. But it also shows that social categories like "black" and "white" are not mutually exclusive, either, that the supposed cultural and psychological barrier between black and white ethnic Americans—symbolized by the long and dangerous ride of Flipper and Cyrus from Harlem to Bensonhurst and back—is just one more myth of American racism. Jungle Fever shows that the relationship between black and white in America is one of endless fascination and cultural and social interpenetration. If whites hate black people, as one character claims, precisely because they want so desperately to be black, then it is also true that black people learned long ago to hate aspects of their cultural selves precisely because the larger society would not, and will not, let them function like (white) people. But the exploitation of the white working class, and Angie's exploitation by the men in her own family, also argue strongly that society creates niggers even in white ethnic havens such as Bensonhurst. Jungle Fever—perhaps destined to be misinterpreted as one more film about white racism—is actually a brilliant exploration of the liminal space that connects, rather than divides, black America with white.

Spike addressing the camera addressing the audience,
introducing *Jungle Fever*.

Wesley Snipes stars in *Jungle Fever*. He plays an architect
from Harlem who leaves his wife for his white, Italian-
American secretary from Bensonhurst. Oh shit!

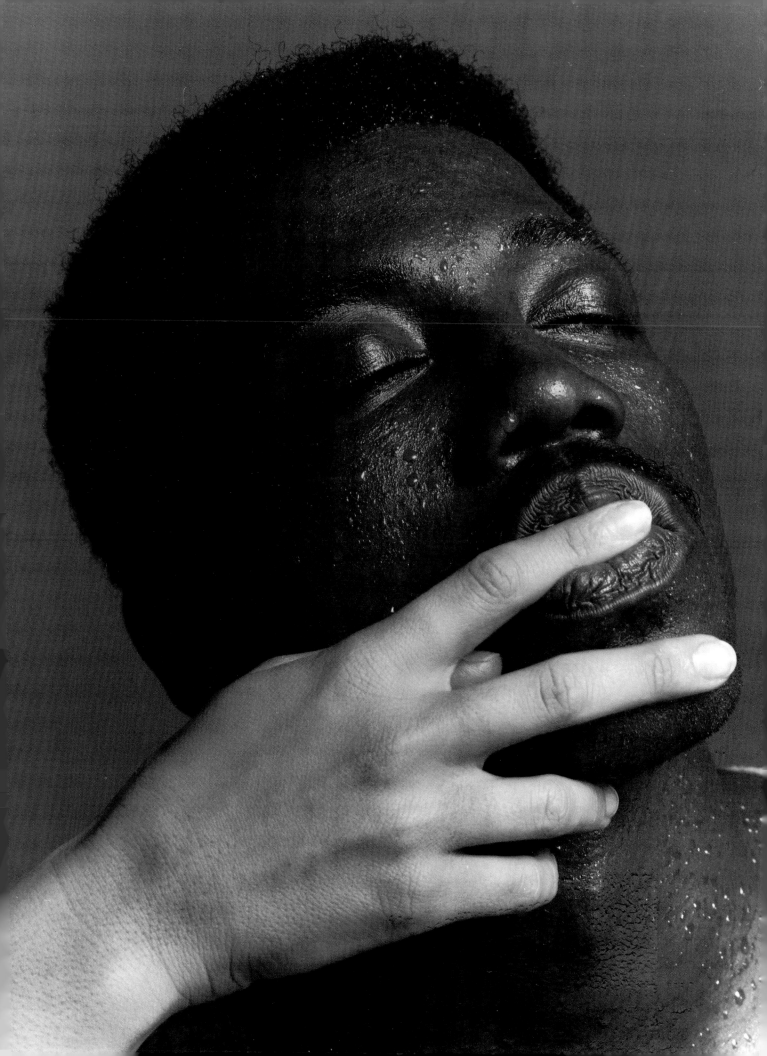

**"Flipper Purify," Wesley Snipes, and "Drew Purify,"
Lonette McGee, ponder the future.**

...eft to right: "Charlie," David Dundara;
...incent; "Angie," Annabella Sciorra;
...nmy," Michael Imperioli.

...onette McGee walks by tracks laid
...vn for the dolly.

"Leslie Covington," Brad Dourif, "Angie," and
"Jerry Mast," Tim Robbins, meet "Flipper"

**Flipper Purify, a struggling black man trying to make it
in a cruel white corporate America.**

**"The Good Reverend Doctor," Ossie Davis. Spike based
the character loosely on Marvin Gaye, Sr.**

Cyrus tries to comfort his "octaroon, quadroon, mulatto" wife, "Vera," Veronica Webb.

Pages 180 and 181: The drafting table scene was the most difficult in the film. Spike recalls, "The sound recordist Russell 'The Oscar' Williams and I had to stuff our ears with Kleenex so the headphones wouldn't burn up as Flipper and Angie did they nasty."

Bensonhurst Rules: the regulars at Lou Carbone's Candy Store. Left to right: "Sonny," Steve Randazzo; "Veeshay," Anthony Nocerino; "Patty," Joe D'Onofrio; "Vinny," Nick Turturro; and "Frankie Botz," Mike Badalucco.

**Sylvia's Restaurant. The crew loved shooting there
that day—no complaints about the food.**

"Vinny" takes his girl "Denise," Debi Mazar, for a spin
through the neighborhood.

Drew throws Flipper's belongings out the window.

VERA: I'm not black, I'm not white, and what difference does it make.

DREW: I don't know when your father is coming home.

Mike's two sons, Charlie and Jimmy, try to hold him back
when he attacks his "nigger-loving" tramp of a daughter.

Angie holds her head in pain.

Facing page: Mike sends Angie flying.

"Sonny."

"Lou Carbone," Anthony Quinn. Quinn was in Rome
when Robi Reed and Spike Lee were casting. It took
many transatlantic phone calls to sign him on.

Brothers from the Fruit of Islam who worked as security
"protect" Debi Mazar.

"Orin," Tyra Ferrell, and admirer, "Paulie,"
John Turturro.

"Lucinda," Ruby Dee, and her son, "Flipper."

"Vivian, the Crack Ho," Halle Berry, accosts "Flipper"
as he walks his daughter "Ming," Veronica Timbers,
to school.

This woman is a real life crack addict. She walked up to
Spike and his crew and offered her technical expertise in
that field. They accepted.

"Gator," Sam Jackson, is Flipper's cracked-out older
brother. He and "Vivian" suck on that
"glass dick."

Pages 196 and 197: The Taj Mahal, world's biggest
crack den, across 110th Street.

Flipper and Angie messing around.

Mistaken identity. Guns are drawn.

Don't Shoot!

Spike, Ernest, and company watch the monitor.

The Good Reverend Doctor reads the riot act to his son:
"Guess who's not coming to dinner."

Pages 202 and 203: Flipper and Angie on opposite sides
of the bed, which might as well be opposite ends
of the world.

Joe Pepitone baseball bats from Bensonhurst.

Hank Aaron *vs.* **Joe Pepitone.**

FRANKIE: **My mother ain't Black, she's just dark.**

VINNY: **What are you doing in our neighborhood?**

PATTY: **You ever heard of Yusuf Hawkins?**

First assistant director, Randy Fletcher; co-producer, Monty Ross; line producer, Jon Kilik; production supervisor, Preston Holmes; and unit manager, Brent Owens.

VIVIAN: Eat me.

GATOR: I need money.

A father shoots his first child.

A mother cradles her son.

Black family destroyed by drugs.

Gun and Bible.

Director on the phone as Gator lies dead on carpet.

"NO!"

The crew (and some cast) from *Jungle Fever*.
That's *Five for Five*.

CONTRIBUTORS

Toni Cade Bambara has published two short story collections, *Gorilla, My Love* and *The Seabirds Are Still Alive*, and a novel, *The Salt Eaters*. She lives in Philadelphia, and scripted and narrated the documentary "The Bombing of Osage Avenue," produced and directed by Louis Massiah.

Henry Louis Gates, Jr. (PhD University of Cambridge, 1979), W. E. B. DuBois Professor of Humanities at Harvard University, taught at Duke, Yale, and Cornell universities before going to Harvard. He is the general editor of the *Norton Anthology of Afro-American Literature*, and the editor of Oxford's thirty-volume series, *The Schomburg Library of Nineteenth Century Black Women Writers*. His publications include *Figures in Black: Words, Signs, and the Racial Self* and *The Signifying Monkey: A Theory of Afro-American Literary Criticism*, which won the American Book Award.

Nelson George is a weekly columnist for *The Village Voice*, a contributor to *Playboy*, and the author of several books including *Where Did Our Love Go? The Rise and Fall of the Motown Sound*, *The Michael Jackson Story*, and *The Death of Rhythm & Blues*. His book about black men in basketball will be published in 1992. He lives in Brooklyn, New York.

Charles Johnson is the Pollock Professor of English at the University of Washington. His recent novel *Middle Passage* won the 1990 National Book Award for fiction and was nominated for a National Book Critics Circle Award. In addition to numerous essays and short stories, he has written a work of aesthetics and criticism, *Being and Race: Black Writing Since 1970*. His novels include *Oxherding Tale*, *Faith and the Good Thing*, and *The Sorcerer's Apprentice*. Professor Johnson was also the script-writer for two PBS films, "Charlie Smith and the Fritter Tree" and "Booker," was the creator of the PBS series "Charlie's Pad," and was a writer-producer on the series "Up and Coming."

Terry McMillan is the author of the novels *Mama* and *Disappearing Acts*, and is also the editor of *Breaking Ice: An Anthology of Contemporary African-American Fiction*. She teaches at the University of Arizona. Her novel *Waiting to Exhale* will be published in 1992.

Melvin Van Peebles was the first black director to create a body of work in modern Hollywood (including the landmark *Sweet Sweetback's Baadasssss Song* and the recent *Identity Crisis*). Van Peebles has been called a "twentieth-century Renaissance man" by the *New York Times*. His career goes beyond producing, writing, directing, and acting for the cinema to include authoring thirteen books (five in French), Broadway and off-Broadway shows (two of which garnered numerous Tony nominations), television specials, a mini-series, plus winning an Emmy in 1987 for his teleplay concerning censorship. He also has been a trader on the American Stock Exchange; his 1986 book (*Bold Money*) explains the intricacies of the option market to the layman. His current projects are *Dirty Pictures* (a novel about long-distance runners and murder) and a one-man off-Broadway show (*Kickin the Science*).

Designed by Jim Wageman

The text, set in Gill Sans Light and Bold,
was composed with QuarkXpress 3.0 on a
Macintosh IIsi and output on a Linotronic L300.

The book was printed and bound by
Toppan Printing Company,
Tokyo, Japan.